Plays in Print
An imprint of Smith and Kraus Publishers, Inc.
Published by Smith and Kraus, Inc.
177 Lyme Road, Hanover, NH 03755
www.SmithandKraus.com

ISBN-13: 978-1-936232-41-3
ISBN-10: 1-936232-41-3

Cover photo: Natalie Berk, Alex Mills and Stacey Jackson
Photography by Scott Suchman

Design and layout: Barry Halvorson

Manufactured in the United States of America

the Liar

Adapted by David Ives
From the comedy by Pierre Corneille

Commissioned by:

SHAKESPEARE THEATRE COMPANY

Artistic Director Michael Kahn
Managing Director Chris Jennings

as part of its ReDiscovery Series

The commissioning and world premiere production of *The Liar*
were made possible by the generous support of
The Beech Street Foundation.

REVISED EDITION

About the Shakespeare Theatre Company

Since its founding in 1985, the Shakespeare Theatre Company has endeavored to be the nation's leading force in the presentation and preservation of classic theatre. The core mission is to present classic theatre in an accessible, skillful, imaginative, American style that honors playwrights' language and intentions while viewing their plays through a 21st-century lens. With the formation of the Harman Center for the Arts — which includes Sidney Harman Hall and the Lansburgh Theatre — the Shakespeare Theatre Company is a national destination theatre offering a broad range of works to audiences in the greater-Washington area and across the nation.

The Shakespeare Theatre Company enjoys national and international renown as "the nation's foremost Shakespeare company" (*The Wall Street Journal*), producing "a repertory of classics that no New York theatre of similar size and scale can match" (*The New York Times*).

For more information about the Shakespeare Theatre Company's artistic programming, nationally acclaimed educational programs and the Free For All — an annual production of free performances for the greater Washington, D.C., community — please visit ShakespeareTheatre.org.

 SHAKESPEARE THEATRE COMPANY
Artistic Director Michael Kahn
Managing Director Chris Jennings

Administrative Offices
516 8ᵗʰ Street SE
Washington, DC 20003

202.547.1122
ShakespeareTheatre.org

About the ReDiscovery Series

During my first season as artistic director of the Shakespeare Theatre Company, we presented four plays. Three came from our namesake playwright, whose works form the basis of any classical theatre's repertoire. But for our fourth production, we chose Niccolo Machiavelli's 1518 play *The Mandrake*, and commissioned a new translation and adaptation of this lesser known play.

Over two decades later the company has seen many changes: we have created landmark productions with some of the English-speaking world's greatest actors, directors and designers, and we have expanded into two theatres in downtown Washington, D.C. to accommodate a growing audience for classic theatre. But even as our reach and ambitions have expanded to six or seven productions in a season, we continue to produce three plays by William Shakespeare annually. The rest come from the vast range of world dramatic writing.

From that first season, we realized that a great classical company can not live on Shakespeare alone. And so the Shakespeare Theatre Company has developed a reputation for artistic risk-taking that has extended beyond re-interpreting the language and time periods of well-known classics to the revival of little-known or neglected works. Our efforts to find and produce those works began in 1994 with the launch of the ReDiscovery Series. In this series, we and our audience investigate exemplary plays of the classical canon that are rarely performed in today's theatre through readings by some of D.C.'s and New York's finest actors. The readings provide audiences with a visual and aural sense of the work, and the combined efforts and responses of artists, scholars and audience illuminate the play's potential and limitations. After 15 seasons, many plays featured in the series have made their way onto our stages, including Musset's *Lorenzaccio*, Euripides' *Ion*, Lope de Vega's *The Dog in the Manger* and Jonson's *The Silent Woman*.

We also believe that to ensure that classical plays—especially forgotten works—remain relevant and accessible to contemporary audiences, they need to be translated and adapted by the best modern writers. Thanks to a path-breaking grant from the Beech Street Foundation, we have begun to commission these new versions. I have always believed that re-introducing these works to modern audiences and the American theatre community is an essential part of our mission in preserving and reinvigorating the classical repertoire. After their world premieres on our stages, therefore, we hope that a steady stream of these plays will find its way onto stages throughout this country. *The Liar* is the first in this series, but by no means the last. Great plays with enduring language and themes are just waiting to be rediscovered.

Michael Kahn
Artistic Director
Shakespeare Theatre Company

The Whole Truth About *The Liar*

David Ives

When my agent called and asked if I'd be interested in translating Corneille's *The Liar* for the Shakespeare Theatre Company of Washington, I had never heard of the play. Nor had he. Not that I was all that *up* on French theatre, though I had recently found myself wading into the tricky waters of translation. Using the remains of my college French and memories of a romantic week in Paris, I had somehow managed translations of Feydeau's *A Flea In Her Ear* and Yasmina Reza's *A Spanish Play* to some success. As it turned out I needn't have been ashamed of my ignorance in the case of *The Liar*. I doubt there were 500 people in this republic of 300 million who knew the piece or even the title.

In any case: "Send the script along," I told my agent. "I'll take a look at it."

He sent, I looked, and several hours later, with the help of a fat French dictionary, I found myself astonished. Exhilarated. Giddy. For, lying on the desk before me, was one of the world's great comedies. I felt as if some lost Shakespeare festival comedy on the order of *Twelfth Night* or *Much Ado about Nothing* had been found. This particular Shakespeare comedy was unfortunately locked away in French (the French have a way of doing things like that), but I could remedy that. The prospect of Englishing this play made me feel like Ronald Colman distantly sighting Shangri-La.

Everything about it spoke to me. The rippling language. The rich simplicity of the premise. The gorgeousness of the set pieces. The seeming insouciance of the treatment alongside the classical rigor of the plotting. The way the play's wide understanding and humanity was nicely seasoned with several large pinches of social satire. *The Liar* is one of those plays that seem to be made out of almost nothing, yet end up being about so much. *The Importance of Being Earnest* comes to mind, and *Hay Fever*. It's one of those plays that are both a view on our world and their own separate world, one that we would happily inhabit.

Corneille (that's pronounced Cor-*nay*, by the way) wrote *Le Menteur* in the middle of his great career as a return to comedy, and it shows. The play has all the ease of a successful playwright completely in control of his powers. He seems to be improvising this *divertissement* before our eyes, riffing on the Spanish play he stole the basic plot from (and which he vastly improved). Though written in Corneille's middle age, *The Liar* sparkles with youth and put me in mind ever after of a poem by Robert Hillyer that Ned Rorem set to music: "Early in the morning / Of a lovely summer day, / As they lowered the bright awning / At the outdoor café, / I was breakfasting on croissants / And café au lait / Under greenery like scenery / Rue François Premier..."

All that being said, I have to add that what you hold in your hand is not... *exactly*...Corneille. For, having been bowled over by the play, I had to consider how to render this luminous world in English. There was one thing that I knew right away: it had to be in verse, just as it is in Corneille.

The Liar is a portrait of a brilliant performer and, language being the wire Dorante dances upon, the language had to match his agile mind at every turn. Prose would have turned this into a "Seinfeld" episode and made it banal. Only rhyme would do.

Next question: translate the whole play, translate some of the play, or make another play "based on" Corneille (like Tony Kushner's version of Corneille's *The Illusion*)? Frankly, there were elements of the plot that did not satisfy me, and which I doubted would satisfy anybody else either: Lucrece was a cipher, indeed virtually a non-speaking role for most of the action; Cliton's relationship to Dorante and to the play's underlying themes wasn't clear; the two maids were thankless parts; and the wrap-up was cursory in the extreme. No offense intended, but the dénouement was very French: Dorante realizes he's gotten his lady love's name wrong and changes his mind, simply plopping for Lucrece and professing his love. Not good enough.

Samuel Johnson once said: "We must try its effect as an English poem; that is the way to judge the merit of a translation." I submit that the same principle applies to plays, especially old ones. In fact, for my money only playwrights should translate plays because the point is not to carry over sentences from one language to another, but to produce a credible, speakable, playable, produceable play for today *no matter what's in the original.* "That's what he wrote in 1643," is no defense. If actors can't play every line, if every moment isn't comedic or dramatic or both – fuhgeddaboutit. Or as the French say, with a shrug: *bfff!*

What you hold in your hand is what I call a translaptation, i.e., a translation with a heavy dose of adaptation. For what I have realized in translating plays is that, in an odd way, the language of a play is of secondary concern. (Just look at the lumbering dialogue of O'Neill, which certainly doesn't obviate incomparable dramatic power.) In translating a play, I contend, one must think as a playwright, not as a translator. One must ask: what is the play *underneath* the words, what is going on *beneath* speeches rather than on their surface, who are these characters and what drives them, and finally what is this play actually all about? What was on Corneille's chest and how can I use what's on mine to create something with dramatic and comedic integrity? It seems to me that that's the only way a translated play can ever have what every good play has to have: a voice.

In other words, you have to write the play Corneille would have written today, in English.

If he were you.

And vice versa.

In the end I did to *The Liar* what Corneille had done to his Spanish source. I ran with it. I trimmed some very long speeches (the French *love them*) and broke up others. I parceled out the action between interiors and exteriors rather than setting most of the action – as "classical" writers implausibly do – in a street. I let Cliton meet Dorante in scene one and gave him a problem with the truth that would complement his boss's problem. I beefed up Lucrece and tried to lend her some personality, since the original part feels like it was written for some talent-free but gobsmackingly beautiful chorine that Corneille was sleeping with. I cut a useless manservant (save the producers some money!) and doubled the maids' parts, making them twins. (More saved money! Use it on costumes!) I added the queen, offstage, and cut some unimportant onstage remarks that many might find politically unacceptable today. Loving duels (who doesn't?) I wrote in the duel which in the original happens offstage. I inserted a lying lesson – the equivalent of the specialty number at the top of virtually every musical's second act – and rejiggered the ending. I gave Philiste a love interest, tying him into the plot more than he was, and along the way I fell in love with Lucrece. (Who wouldn't?)

Of the three great 17th-century French playwrights – Corneille, Racine, Molière – I'm fondest of Corneille. He seems to me to have the largest heart and the most humanity, great as those other two are. He loves the world in a way those two don't, and this gives him, for me, a Shakespearean understanding and comprehensiveness. In that imaginary game of What Writers Would You Invite To Dinner, Corneille would be on my list rather than the others because Racine would pick at his food (after murmuring a pious grace over it) and suck up to the celebrities while Molière would hog Shakespeare all to himself to bitch about box office receipts and the loxes in his audience. I'd seat Corneille between the elfin essayist Charles Lamb, who would delight him, and Horace, who would hymn the waitress in deathless hexameters and keep all their glasses filled.

The truth, the whole truth and nothing but the truth, as refracted in a theatrical fun-house mirror. Welcome to *The Liar.*

About David Ives

David Ives is probably best known for his evenings of one-act plays called *All in the Timing* and *Time Flies*. Recent shows include *New Jerusalem: The Interrogation of Baruch de Spinoza*; Irving Berlin's *White Christmas*; *Is He Dead?* (adapted from Mark Twain); and *Venus in Fur*. He is the author of three young-adult novels, *Monsieur Eek*, *Scrib*, and *Voss*. He is a graduate of Yale School of Drama and a former Guggenheim Fellow in playwriting.

About Pierre Corneille

As the eldest son and namesake of Pierre Corneille, a lawyer and administrator in the French city of Rouen, the young Pierre Corneille was expected to become a Rouen lawyer and administrator himself. Born in 1606, he showed tremendous academic promise and dutifully studied law in college. But he was a tongue-tied litigator, and felt more inclined to write poetry than to practice law. So his father used his connections to set up young Corneille at the Rouen Department of Forests and Rivers.

Bored at work, he began to write plays in his spare time. His first, a comedy called *Mélite*, came to the attention of a touring company on its way to Paris. The play was a surprise hit, and he followed it up with five more successful comedies. These plays gained him a very powerful patron in Paris: Cardinal Richelieu, Chief Minister to King Louis XIII. The Cardinal invited Corneille to join "The Society of the Five Authors," a group of playwrights commissioned to write exclusively for the Cardinal. Expected to produce plays that expressed the Cardinal's moral standards, however, Corneille felt stifled by the restrictions, and returned to his hometown of Rouen in 1635.

Freed from constraint, Corneille experienced a burst of creativity. He wrote his first tragedy, *Medée*, the wildly experimental comedy *The Theatrical Illusion*, and his masterpiece, the genre-defying history play *The Cid*. A colossal success with audiences (including the King), this play about the tension between love and duty nevertheless drew the ire of Richelieu's newly-incorporated French Academy, which attacked it for not conforming to moral standards or to the so-called "classical unities." The hailstorm of criticism drove Corneille from playwriting in 1637, and he resolved to return to his old post in Rouen and to start a family.

By 1640, however, Corneille began to write for the theatre again, if more cautiously. His new works were almost exclusively tragedies, and they hewed much closer to the Academy's established rules. *Horace*, *Cinna*, and *Polyeucte* all told stories from Ancient Rome, and followed the classical conventions by transpiring over a single day at a single location. These serious-minded tragedies promoted honor and virtue above all else.

In the midst of this more serious turn, Corneille unexpectedly produced his comic masterpiece, *The Liar*, in 1643. Based on *The Suspicious Truth* by the Mexican-Spanish playwright Juan Ruiz de Alarcón, it also seems drawn in part from Corneille's own life. Just as Corneille left the law in provincial Rouen for the romantic life of an artist in Paris, so the young liar/lawyer Dorante leaves his legal studies in Poitiers for romance in the big city.

Perhaps more importantly, Corneille's play revolutionized the idea of what French comedy could be. Instead of the Italian-style farce that had previously dominated the stage, Corneille's comedies aimed at depicting the foibles of the upper class with up-to-the-minute accuracy. This led to a higher style of language and plotting, and to a sense of contemporary relevance. His stylish verse brought comedy into a parallel, rather than inferior, relationship to tragedy.

Now married to Marie de Lampérière, with whom he would have seven children, Corneille saw his popularity slowly wane. In 1652, after his newest play flopped and he lost his patronage, Corneille left the theatre. The promise of a new patron, the finance minister Nicolas Fouquet, finally drew him back to writing plays in 1659. Heartened by the success of his tragedy *Oedipe*, Corneille moved his family to Paris. In 1663, he began to receive a pension from the king, and he wrote new tragedies nearly every year. Beginning in 1664, he gained a formidable rival, the brash young playwright Jean Racine. Racine wrote searing emotional tragedies, and the older Corneille struggled to keep up.

Though Corneille's later plays met with little success, he remained a respected figure, and his early plays were frequently revived. And his influence on the course of French play-writing can not be ignored. The same year Corneille wrote *The Liar*, a 21-year-old Parisian named Jean-Baptiste Poquelin founded his first theatre. When he later wrote his own plays (under the name Molière), he absorbed many of Corneille's techniques to craft hilarious and cutting satires on French society. "We owe Molière to *The Liar*," wrote the writer and philosopher Voltaire. Corneille's comic subjects and style influenced not only Molière, but also his great successors Marivaux and Beaumarchais. Corneille died in 1684, but his legacy lived on.

Akiva Fox
Literary Associate
Shakespeare Theatre Company

Corneille *IN A MINUTE*

AGE	YEAR	
	1606	Enter Pierre Corneille.
3	1609	Johann Carolus of Germany publishes the 'Relation', the first newspaper.
4	1610	Upon the death of King Henry IV of France, his son Louis XIII becomes king at age nine.
6	1612	Marin le Bourgeoys creates the first flintlock musket for Louis XIII.
12	1618	The Thirty Years' War begins, involving most of Europe in crippling conflict.
18	1624	Cardinal Richelieu becomes prime minister to King Louis XIII, centralizing the power of the state as never before.
23	1629	Corneille – *Mélite*
28	1634	Corneille – *The Place Royale*
30	1636	Pedro Calderón de la Barca – *Life is a Dream*
30	1636	Corneille – *The Theatrical Illusion*
31	1637	Corneille – *The Cid*
34	1640	Corneille – *Horace*
35	1641	René Descartes publishes *Meditations on First Philosophy*. Corneille – *Cinna*
36	1642	A civil war breaks out in England as a result of a dispute between the parliament and King Charles I
37	1643	Upon the death of King Louis XIII, his son Louis XIV becomes king at age five. Corneille – *The Liar*

Corneille *IN A MINUTE*, cont.

AGE	YEAR	
42	1648	The Peace of Westphalia ends the Thirty Years' War and the Eighty Years' War, marking the ends of Spain and the Holy Roman Empire as major European powers. In response to the raising of taxes, a civil war known as the Fronde breaks out in Paris
46	1652	Corneille retires from the theatre after *Pertharite* receives poor reviews.
47	1653	Blaise Pascal publishes *Treatise on the Arithmetical Triangle*.
53	1659	Corneille returns to the stage with *Oedipe*.
55	1661	Upon the death of his prime minister Cardinal Mazarin, Louis XIV takes on personal control of France.
58	1664	Molière – *Tartuffe*
60	1666	Molière – *The Misanthrope*
64	1670	French monk Dom Perignon creates champagne. Corneille – *Tite et Bérénice* Racine – *Bérénice*
65	1671	Corneille and Molière – *Psyché*
71	1677	Racine – *Phèdre*
76	1682	La Salle explores the length of the Mississippi River and claims Louisiana for France.
78	1684	Exit Pierre Corneille.

Critical acclaim for *The Liar*:

"*The Liar* and its mischievous adapter, David Ives, want you to savor every meticulously groomed conceit, every stylishly turned-out couplet, every assiduously manicured joke. Ives is an inveterate jester, a trait that serves him well on an evening that is all jest."

The Washington Post

"If there's anything half as entertaining as *The Liar* onstage hereabouts, I'd be obliged if someone would let me know about it."

Washington City Paper

"Michael Kahn's robust staging of *The Liar* whips past at high-speed, like spun sugar gathered from a cotton candy machine... a scrubbed, vivacious script salted with hints of cheeky self-awareness."

DC Theatre Scene

"Astonishingly fresh, funny and totally appealing to modern audiences."

The Washington Examiner

This adaptation of *The Liar* was first performed by the Shakespeare Theatre Company at the Lansburgh Theatre in Washington D.C., where it opened on April 12, 2010 under the direction of Michael Kahn.

This updated, finalized version of the script reflects the revisions made during the rehearsal process.

Original cast:

DORANTE
Christian Conn*

GERONTE
David Sabin*

CLITON
Adam Green*

CLARICE
Erin Partin*

LUCRECE
Miriam Silverman*

ALCIPPE
Tony Roach*

PHILISTE
Aubrey Deeker*

ISABELLE/SABINE
Colleen Delany*

* Member of Actors' Equity Association, the Union of Professional Actors and Stage Managers.

Original production team:

Director
Michael Kahn

Set Designer
Alexander Dodge

Costume Designer
Murell Horton

Lighting Designer
Jeff Croiter

Composer
Adam Wernick

Sound Designer
Martin Desjardins

Voice and Dialects
Ellen O'Brien

Assistant Director
Alan Paul

Literary Associate
Akiva Fox

Stage Manager
M. William Shiner*

Assistant Stage Manager
Elizabeth Clewley*

Casting
Stuart Howard, Amy Schecter & Paul Hardt

* Member of Actors' Equity Association, the Union of Professional Actors and Stage Managers.

THE CHARACTERS:

DORANTE
a young man just arrived in Paris

GERONTE
Dorante's father

CLITON
Dorante's servant

CLARICE
a young lady of Paris

LUCRECE
Clarice's best friend

ALCIPPE
Clarice's secret fiancé

PHILISTE
Alcippe's friend

ISABELLE
vivacious servant to Lucrece

SABINE
puritanical servant to Clarice

Note: Isabelle and Sabine are
played by the same actress.

The setting is Paris in 1643.

This play's for Jay
(Binder, of course,
casting's lord)
whom gay Corneille
would have adored.

—David Ives

ACT ONE

Scene One.

(The actor playing CLITON appears before the curtain.)

CLITON ACTOR

Ladies and gentlemen! Mesdames, messieurs!
All cell phones off? All cellophane secure?
Finish your texting now, not during my scene.
"I'm in some theatre. But, like, where's the screen?"
No eating, please. You think you're incognito?
Yes, you. The lady with the bean burrito.
Put it away. I have a crucial message!
(Points to a man in the audience.)
This guy looks worried. "Whoa, what does *this* presage?"
I paid my fifty bucks, sprang for a cab,
Another twenty plus the dinner tab,
We had to chug-a-lug that nice Bordeaux,
I hoped I'd be asleep by now, but no,
Some bird comes on at, what's it, eight-oh-eight,
Prob'ly to say, *"We're running slightly late..."*
Well, set your minds at ease, reduce the strain,
And with your iPods, please — turn off your brain.
Leave complications to our evening's hero,
A lying genius, if a moral zero.
No, my announcement may be even worse:
Tonight our actors will be speaking verse!
In case you hadn't noticed that small fact.
We'll speak PENTAMETER, to be exact.
And what the blank's pentameter, you say?
It's what I'm speaking now! On with the play!
(He picks up a sign that says: "RENT ME! CLITON. SERVANT FOR HIRE." He raps the staff on the stage three times and our scene is revealed.)
The Paris gardens of Les Tuilleries —
A fine spring day in 1643.
Servant! Servant for hire! Get your servant here!
(DORANTE enters, with sword drawn, in an outfit whose cuffs and collar are trimmed with lots of lace.)

DORANTE

En garde!
(CLITON hits the dirt with a cry.)

Arise, you knave! Come, stand and fight!

CLITON
Sweet Jesus, sir. I almost soiled my tights!

DORANTE
(Fencing positions.)
First. Second. Third. And parry. Lunge. *Allez!*
Am I in first?

CLITON
That's fourth, sir — in ballet.

DORANTE
I like your honesty.

CLITON
It's all I've got.
D'ya need a man? I'm cheap. C'mon, take a shot.
I don't eat much. Check my diameter.
I cook, I clean, I speak pentameter...

DORANTE
(Points off left.)
I'll ponder it upon the Elysées.

CLITON
(Points off right.)
Champs Elysées, my friend, lies that-a-way,
Unless the Louvre has mouvred since yesterday.
Just got to town?

DORANTE
Two hours.

CLITON
                    No.

DORANTE
                    Yes! Poitiers —
That's where I come from. Near Poitiers, I mean.
A lovely spot...

CLITON
(The exposition scene.)

DORANTE
I studied law there, but I got so bored

I clamored for a scabbard and a sword.
At last my Dad reluctantly agreed
And we converged on Paris with all speed —
He to procure me some prosaic wife,
I to pursue the soldier's life. So now
Begone, dull briefs, you legal pillory!
For here I stand within the Twillery
Where ladies buzz and fancy dandies dart
And high society comes by the cart.
This Parisian patina. Air like ice.
My dreams have not deceived me. It's paradise!

CLITON

(Dubious:)
Mmm.

DORANTE

But tell me frankly. Do I look the part?
Does this display say "military ace"?

CLITON

Uh, no, it's more like, "wheredja get the lace?"

DORANTE

One wants a style, a character, a code,
An up-to-date persona à la mode.

CLITON

I'll tell you what you need: a personal guide,
One part valet and one part...
(Rips off some of Dorante's lace.)
                              ...pesticide.
The key to living here with proper flash?
Same secret you'll find everyplace.

DORANTE
                    Um...

CLITON
                    Cash.
Just watch how you deploy it. Meanwhile, enjoy it!
And, hey. You're young, you're free, so have no fear.
Stupider guys than you have made it here.

DORANTE

You're very blunt. I thought you sought a place.

CLITON
You think I'm gabbing here to please Your Grace?
You wanted my opinion. What's the matter?

DORANTE
It's not a minion's job to fawn and flatter?

CLITON
Why don't I truckle? Huh? I'll tell you why.
My tragic flaw: I cannot tell a lie.
Come on and test me. Put me in duress.
Ask me if I've ever stolen.

DORANTE
              Have y...?

CLITON
                      Yes.
The same thing fifty times has come to pass:
My boss asks me the truth, then fires my ass.
You chuckle?

DORANTE
       Not at all.

CLITON
              Well, you inquired.

DORANTE
You could be just the man I need. You're hired.
(Shake hands.)
Dorante.

CLITON
       Cliton. You won't regret this, sire.
Now how about a petty cash advance?

DORANTE
Of course!
(Realizes:)
My money's in my other pants.

CLITON
No prob. Your mug's as trusty as the map of France.
(Truth is — he's lying, but I don't know it yet.
Will I find out in time? You wanna bet?)
And your first wish, amongst the joys of Hades?

DORANTE
Tell me about your celebrated ladies.
Do they succumb, or are they hard to please?

CLITON
You just arrived in town, you want a squeeze?

DORANTE
I wouldn't mind one. Where would I find one?

CLITON
It's only 9 a.m. Boy, you work fast!
I gather you have women in your past?

DORANTE
I've had adventures with the tender sex.
There was my time with — let's say "Princess X."
That night at Cannes with her pet cockatoo...
But you don't want to hear.

CLITON
                              Oh, yes, I do!
Just stay away from this town's hotter blends.
You'll only burn your handle at both ends.
What you want is a socialite with spice,
A vestal virgin not averse to vice.
(CLARICE and LUCRECE enter, followed by Lucrece's maid, ISABELLE.)

DORANTE
But soft. Who're these fair dames?

CLITON
                                    They're not my class.
These two are sterling. I commune with brass.

DORANTE
(To CLARICE, taking her hand.)
Watch out there, mademoiselle! The pavement's tipped.
What luck I caught your hand or you'd have tripped.
No, don't let go. Your stumble was a sign.
O sov'reign joy to hold your hand in mine!

CLARICE
However sweet your manual sensation,
This hand's not meant, monsieur, for your palpation.

DORANTE

'Tis true, 'twas fickle fortune made us meet.
And that's what makes these digits bittersweet.
This prize is won yet I'd more happily bear it
If I had gained this prize through my own merit.

CLARICE

But, sir, a favor won is merely favor bought.
As happiness is happiest unsought.

DORANTE

Yet effort may enhance the unforeseen.
(Bends to kiss her hand.)
To prove the point, let effort intervene —

LUCRECE

Ah-hem!

DORANTE

Your mute friend disagrees. Or does she scoff?

CLARICE

Oh, she means nothing, sir.

LUCRECE

Ah-*hem!*

CLARICE

The whooping cough.

Where were we?

DORANTE

You had lent me this rich alm.
But let me touch your heart, not just your palm.
(DORANTE bends again to kiss her hand.)

LUCRECE

AH-*HEM!*
(LUCRECE pulls CLARICE away, to speak aside.)

CLARICE

Excuse me, please.

LUCRECE

(Clarice, you could be *seen*.)

CLARICE

(Oh, peace, Lucrece. Be seen by whom?)

LUCRECE

(Alcippe.)

CLARICE

(Alcippe's asleep. So why so dubious?)

LUCRECE

(*Clarice*. Your fiancé's *Vesuvius*.)

CLARICE

(So let him spew. My lover's lava's nothing new.
Two years now we've been secretly engaged —
And *he's* the one who's chronically enraged?
Oh, very well.)

A pleasure, sir. Adieu.

DORANTE

O, shatter, tortured soul! O, break, my heart!
Endure these weeks of fire, to see us part?

CLARICE

These weeks, you say? I must have missed a spark.
Of your existence I've been in the dark.

DORANTE

You mean you haven't seen me haunt your door
Since I returned from fighting in the war?

CLITON

(The war?)

CLARICE

The war...?

DORANTE

Six months ago.

CLITON

(Six *months?*)

DORANTE

Artillery captain on the German front.
Ja! Spilling crimson streams I fought the Hun
At Leberwurst, Heissfrankfurter, and so on.
Four years of hell. But King and France required me.

CLITON

(Is this the self-same simpleton who hired me?)

DORANTE

The siege of Zinkendorf, up on the walls,
I took not one but ten Teutonic balls.
That's how I got this scar along my jaw...

CLITON

(What scar?)

DORANTE

(Shut up.)

CLITON

(I thought you studied law!)

DORANTE

You may have read my name in the Gazette.
I caused, if not some buzz, then a buzz-ette.
That little dust-up north of Waterloo —
But you don't want to hear...

CLARICE

Oh, yes, I do!

DORANTE

The wounds are almost healed, the pain's abating...

CLITON

(Monsieur, did you know you're hallucinating?)

DORANTE

But then last year while here on winter leave
By chance I glimpsed a corner of your sleeve
In a coach window passing on the Pont Neuf.
It was eneuf, that innocent lace ceuf.
I gave up arms — for leuf!

CLITON

(Is this a dream?)

DORANTE

Yes, I who coolly spilled those crimson streams,
Now wept! Forgive me, goddess, if I'm fervent.
For six long months I've lived to be...
(Kisses her hand.)

...your servant.

ISABELLE

(To LUCRECE:)
(Madame! Alcippe!)

LUCRECE

(Alcippe!)

CLARICE

(Alcippe?)

LUCRECE

(He's on the way.)

CLARICE

Perhaps we'll meet again, monsieur. Good day.

DORANTE

(Hanging onto her hand.)
You'd go so soon, my treasure? Just like that?

CLARICE

I have no leisure for a longer chat.
Let go, monsieur! You've had your conversation!

DORANTE

But give me leave.

CLARICE

For what?

DORANTE

For adoration,
To love you, worship you. Please! I implore!

CLARICE

True lovers ask no leave. They just adore.
(CLARICE and LUCRECE exit. ISABELLE lingers, winking at CLITON.)

DORANTE

Go chase the maid, Cliton. Find out her name.

CLITON

The maid's?

DORANTE

The mistress, fool!

CLITON

(To ISABELLE:)

A word, madame.

ISABELLE

My name is Isabelle, I'm twenty-eight.
Okay, I'm twenty-nine. I'm single, straight,
Catholic, but please don't let that interfere.
I like Italian food and English beer.
Stuffed animals, long walks, Chanel perfume.
Here's my address and the key to my room.
(She holds out a key.)

CLITON

To tell the truth...

ISABELLE

What's wrong? Not feeling sinful?

CLITON

Me? All the time. But it's your lady's info
I wanted. Name, address, any old fact.
Her personal data.

ISABELLE

Hey, what is this? Tact?
I'm not attractive? Not a perfect ten?

CLITON

Maybe an eight.
(She slaps him.)

That tragic flaw again!

ISABELLE

My lady's name's Lucrece. She's filthy rich.

CLITON

Primo. But wait a sec. So there's no glitch —
Those two who just were here — your lady's which?

ISABELLE

The greater beauty.

CLITON

Yeah, terrific, but

Specifically...?

ISABELLE

Okay, then, it's your loss.
(She's about to drop the key in her dress.)

CLITON

Wait, wait, wait, wait — and her address? Your boss?

ISABELLE

She and her friend are neighbors on the Ploss.

CLITON

The "Ploss"? Is that some clue?

ISABELLE

The Place *Royale*.

LUCRECE

(Offstage:)
Isabelle!
(ISABELLE drops the key down her dress.)

ISABELLE

Maybe next time. Sorry, pal. Adieu.
(ISABELLE exits.)

DORANTE

Well?

CLITON

Quote: "The greater beauty of the two
Is named Lucrece." I leave the choice to you.

DORANTE

No contest there. It must be my enchanter.
The cutie who subdued me with her banter.
For beauty, she's the one who won the Fleece.
I feel it in my sternum. She's Lucrece.

CLITON

No disrespect to master's magic throat.
The shy one with the cough would get my vote.

DORANTE

That sphinx? The statue with the delphic stare?
That nun? That lox? The prettier of the pair?

CLITON

Your chatterbox might be Bernice, Therese, Felice...

For pulchritude? The quiet one's Lucrece.

DORANTE

Quiet? She's catatonic! She's amnesia!
The Venus whom I fell for — *she's* Lucretia.

CLITON

If you ask me...?

DORANTE

Cliton, not one more peep!
(Voices, off.)
But who's this here? My ancient friend Alcippe!

CLITON

Looks like your friend's in quite a state.
(ALCIPPE enters in heated conversation with PHILISTE. DORANTE draws CLITON away while ALCIPPE and PHILISTE confer alone.)

ALCIPPE

I *saw* Clarice. She just went through that gate.

PHILISTE

Alcippe, dear boy, *control*. Why so irate?

ALCIPPE

Because last night my servant, very late,
Observed Clarice slip out her own back door
And jump into a waiting coach. What's more?
She wore her diamond gown, her ermine coat.
He followed to the river, where a boat
Awaited, fixed with music, food, divan,
And (let-me-get-my-hands-on-him) a man.

PHILISTE

Oh, Lord. It was another girl, disguised!

ALCIPPE

He saw her float away with his own eyes!
I'm going to find this swine and make him bleed.

DORANTE

Alcippe...?

ALCIPPE

Dorante? Ah, just the friend I need!
(They embrace and do a special handshake.)

You know Philiste? The beau monde's favorite beau?

DORANTE
The man they call the Baron Comme Il Faut?
We know each other from Poitiers.

PHILISTE
Monsieur,
A peerless and unparalleled *plaiseur*.

DORANTE
You two seemed deep in dish.

PHILISTE
Don't start. He's bitter.

DORANTE
Well, well. Some juicy gossip? What's the twitter?

ALCIPPE
A lady serenaded by some fresh gallánt.

DORANTE
Last night?

ALCIPPE
That's right.

PHILISTE
I tell you, stop, Dorante.

DORANTE
No, let me guess. This amorous escapade
Involved... a moonlight picnic with the jade?

ALCIPPE
How did you know that?

DORANTE
And to clinch their joy,
A voyage down the Seine with ships ahoy?

ALCIPPE
Yes, how'd you know...?

DORANTE
An age-old ploy.
Water's like kerosene on Cupid's flame.
And no one knows the happy Don Juan's name?

The backer of this bacchanalian jaunt?

ALCIPPE

Why do you smile...? Not *you?*

DORANTE
'Twas I. Dorante.

Why do you frown?

ALCIPPE
Yes, but... You just got into town!

DORANTE

Oh, I've been here a year...

CLITON
(A year?)

DORANTE
...or less.

I'd certainly be lacking in finesse
If after all this time I lacked success
Locating succubi.

CLITON
(Is this a lie?)

ALCIPPE

But you were speaking of this "bacchanal..."

DORANTE

Since you're my friend, Alcippe, I'll tell you all.

CLITON

(Monsieur, if I were you right now? *Postpone.*)

DORANTE

The barge we lay in like a burnished throne
Burned on the water. Soft music stoked our fire —
Two boats before us with cathedral choir,
And two behind with woodwinds, strings and brass.
I felt that hiring more would be too crass.
But how their plaintive harmonies caressed
The balmy air, as melodies tumesced
And voices mixed in tender competition!
They played a suite of my own composition.
We two reclined meanwhile and sucked moist figs

Within a baldachin of willow twigs
Enlaced with jasmine, while, like circling planets,
Five blindfold virgins served us pomegranates
On alabaster plates. I won't repeat
The panoply of sweets that stained our sheets
(And us) as we lolled there. I won't recall
The dinner courses, no, you'd be appalled.
There were fifteen. A roast, a pig, a calf,
A tumid cock, Lafite in our carafe...
Enough! The list would render you inert.
But then milady offered as dessert
Whipped cream licked from her navel's humid valley.
Then — as a small postprandial finale —
A thousand skyrockets rise up and zoom
From every ark! They penetrate the gloom,
Then, moaning, spill their luminescent spume
Into the wombing dark, their falling embers
Gilding her bare, enthralling, sprawling members
Like golden peelings of some cherub's tangerine...
Then prudish night called "curtain" on the scene.
We danced and fondled till the jasmine drooped
And jealous Sun dispersed our happy troupe.
We parted at the call of Chanticleer,
And mere reality deposited me here.

ALCIPPE

So you're the one.

DORANTE

'Fraid so.

ALCIPPE

The foul seducer.

DORANTE

You'd like the wench. Sometime I'll introduce her.

PHILISTE

That feast would cost the substance of a king!

DORANTE

Philiste, I had an hour to plan this fling.
A small flotilla, yes, but worth the prices.
The lady melted faster than the cherry ices.

ALCIPPE
(As PHILISTE holds him back:)
(How could he be in town a full year's lease
And not know my connection to Clarice?)

PHILISTE
(Alcippe, control yourself. It's all a lie.)

ALCIPPE
(Don't come between us or you also die.)
(To DORANTE:)
You. I. Why. Never. When I. But. *Goodbye!*
(ALCIPPE exits.)

PHILISTE
He had some personal things to clarify.
Alcippe...!
(PHILISTE exits.)

DORANTE
He seemed upset.

CLITON
Upset? I'm terrified!
But sir, could I request a word or twain?

DORANTE
Ask anything you like.

CLITON
Are you insane?

DORANTE
I'm sorry, I don't see...

CLITON
The German front,
Zum Beispiel. Were you really once a grunt
At Schinkenhasenpfefferdinkendorm?

DORANTE
You know how ladies love a uniform.
Just reel off any military muddle,
The dame will deliquesce into a puddle.
In time you share these private lovers' codes.
You just say "Germany" and she explodes.

CLITON
And what about this blow-out on your yacht?
A regatta straight outta Camelot.
"Five Boats, One Woman, or: Don Juan's Thanksgiving."

DORANTE
Cliton, the unimagined life's not worth living.
When someone's got a juicy tale to dish,
I have to add some sauce, re-spice the fish.
A man starts spooning tales of sweet amour
I have to make that man my *dupe du jour*.
(GERONTE enters.)

GERONTE
Dorante, what are you doing, standing idle?

DORANTE
(My Dad.)

GERONTE
You know my business here.

DORANTE
To bridle?

GERONTE
Exactly. No. Though *bridle* is well said
In this case, as we must locate a well-bred
Bride in this place to which you've dragged your sire.
And I've found just the girl whom you require.
I'm on my way to meet her now. A dame
Of high society, of wealth, of name.

CLITON
(Why not just tell about the gal you met?)

DORANTE
(Oh, let him dance his harmless minuet.
I'll sidestep any charmless fiancée.)

GERONTE
What's this? A beggar?

DORANTE
No, my new valet.

CLITON

"A *beggar?*"

GERONTE

"A *valet?*"

DORANTE

Years of experience.

GERONTE

With what?

DORANTE

Some high-placed Presbyterians.
But didn't you say you're off to make my marriage?

GERONTE

And your plans for today?

DORANTE

The royal carriage

Just passed...

GERONTE

No!

DORANTE

Yes. The damn thing came this close.
The sleepy driver, nearly comatose
Happened to graze my boot. We heard a crunch.
No harm done, but the Queen's asked me to brunch.

GERONTE

The Queen?!

DORANTE

I had to say yes, to placate her.

GERONTE

(Hugs him.)
My boy, you're on your way!

DORANTE

Let's catch up later!

(GERONTE exits.)

CLITON

In this town, they will put you through a sieve.

DORANTE
My friend, the thing I'm not will make me live.
But all this chatter's kept me from Lucrece.
That girl is going to be my masterpiece,
My coup, and I won't rest till she's my wife.
Now come and learn the way to spin your life.
(They start out. As they go:)

CLITON
What about my cash advance?

DORANTE
                    Tomorrow.

CLITON
Is that a lie? Are you lying? *Are you lying...?*
(They exit.)

Scene Two.

(Clarice's drawing room. CLARICE and GERONTE confer while LUCRECE and ISABELLE attend in the background.)

GERONTE

You won't be disappointed, mademoiselle.
My son is handsome, tall, he speaks quite well.
And just to show he's not a travesty —
He's brunching right now with Her Majesty!

CLARICE

Brunch? With the Queen?

GERONTE

    He cannot tell a lie.

CLARICE

She never brunches — and is in Versailles.

GERONTE

If you once met my son, you wouldn't doubt him.
His love of fact's the foremost fact about him.
He's youthful but he's truthful, that's Dorante.

CLARICE

I'm sure your son's a gem, Monsieur Geronte,
He's of your family and shares your breed.
But...

GERONTE

   Not to fear. Your uncle has agreed.
The two of us were friends at school, you know.
We talked of you two marrying long ago.
We only lack your voice.

CLARICE

     To be your choice
Honors me indeed. But, Monsieur Geronte,
I fear I'd need to be a clairvoyante
To marry sight-unseen your son...?
(She can't recall the name.)

GERONTE

     Dorante.

CLARICE

                                        Dorante.

It also shows a most unseemly lust
To have a husband. Tell me, is this just:
Could you devise a way for me to see him?
A covert glimpse someday at the museum?

GERONTE

"Someday," Madame Clarice?

CLARICE

                        Next month, next year...

GERONTE

You can examine him today, right here
Beneath your window! When the clock strikes three
I'll draw him to your street and you shall see
My son — or his extern — to your content.
I have no doubt you'll give your quick consent.
Dorante's my only child, and what a prize.

CLARICE

I'll see him first, and then let's rhapsodize.
Till three, then.

GERONTE

                He's reliable, faithful, steady...

CLARICE

Fear not, monsieur. I love the man already.

GERONTE

Mamselle.
(To LUCRECE:)
                Mamselle.
(GERONTE exits.)

LUCRECE

                You may go home now, Isabelle.
(ISABELLE exits.)

CLARICE

Well, fine. Let's vet this mystery candidate.

LUCRECE

You'd quit Alcippe?

CLARICE
Alcippe's two years too late.
Though this... oh, what's his name...

LUCRECE
Dorante.

CLARICE
Sounds like an idiot. And I don't mean *savant*.
I wouldn't want, because of this palaver,
To honeymoon with some jejune cadaver.
Lucrece, oh, please, don't look at me like that.
Of course I'd take Alcippe, just drop a hat.
Or get his gouty father here from Ghent
And wring from him the requisite consent.
I want a husband, cuz.

LUCRECE
You're telling *me*?

CLARICE
And *you're* the gem, you darling. *You* should be
The bride, not I.

LUCRECE
In truth, I've lost all hope.
For I can see without a microscope
That I'm as worthy of a first-class mate
As other women. Yet I stand and wait.
Because I'm silent — all right, call it nervous —
Most men just never see beneath my surface.

CLARICE
Most men can't read you like a crystal ball
Because most men are surface — and that's all.
Though surfaces are nice, in their own way....

LUCRECE
You mean that surface that we met today?

CLARICE
If this man's son is half as prettily wrapped,
I'll scoop him up and sell Alcippe for scrap.
But how'll I tell if he's a tower or a basement
By seeing his surface from my parlor casement?
We women know that looks are error-prone,

Having to please men's eyes but doubt our own.

LUCRECE

An epigram?

CLARICE

No, verbal diarrhea.
But wait a moment. I have an idea!
You haven't a volcanic fiancé.
What if you wrote this son a note? You say
You've noticed him somehow and you desire
A private chat, but you require *discretion*.
Some way to meet without transgression.
(Calls:)
Sabine! — I know! Across your garden gate,
Shrouded by tactful night. So make it late.

LUCRECE

But how....

CLARICE

I speak as you. You hold your peace.
He'll think I'm you — i.e., some girl, "Lucrece."
I find out what he is and what he's not.
Alcippe will never know.

LUCRECE

I like this plot!
And I address this how?

CLARICE

"To My Adonis."

LUCRECE

He'll think I'm joking.

CLARICE

No, he'll think you're honest.
Sabine!
*(SABINE enters. She is played by the same actress who played
ISABELLE but is a sterner, stricter presence.)*

SABINE

Madame?

CLARICE

Sabine, there's going to be a letter.

LUCRECE
As courier, might Isabelle be better?

CLARICE
What difference when our two soubrettes are twins?

SABINE
Madame, I hope this note's no cause for sin.
My sister Isabelle may feed your plots...

CLARICE
No need, Sabine, to tie yourself in knots.

SABINE
You know I'll not promote lubricity.

CLARICE
You can deliver this without duplicity.
But, please, go easy on the rough detergent?

SABINE
Monsieur Alcippe is here. He says it's urgent.

CLARICE
Uh-oh. That means Mount Etna is emergent.

ALCIPPE
(Offstage:)
Clarice!

CLARICE
Come back at three, we'll vet this — damn...

LUCRECE
                                        Dorante.

CLARICE
                                                Dorante!

("Mwah." "Mwah." LUCRECE and SABINE exit.)

ALCIPPE
(Offstage:)
Clarice! Clarice!
(ALCIPPE enters.)

ALCIPPE
You Jezebel! Avaunt!

CLARICE

Now what's all this? Stop growling. Speak your piece.

ALCIPPE

O faithless, fickle, fraudulent Clarice!
Avaunt, I say! My once-prospective spouse!

CLARICE

I can't avaunt, Alcippe. This is my house.

ALCIPPE

Clarice, Clarice...!

CLARICE

Will you stop baying my name like some remonstrance?

ALCIPPE

I only hope that you've ransacked your conscience.

CLARICE

Now what's the matter, pug? Why all these sighs?

ALCIPPE

Oh, why these sighs, you say? Why all these *lies?*
This mask of guiltlessness, this fictive frown?

CLARICE

Speak lower, please. My uncle might come down.

ALCIPPE

Your uncle? Ha! And last night was he ailing
While you were very publicly out sailing?

CLARICE

Sailing?

ALCIPPE

                    While you were boating on the Seine
And sucking figs? Did "uncle" come down then
Or interrupt you in the midst of sin
To rip you from your jasmine *baldachin?*

CLARICE

I'm sorry. What's a baldachin, again?

ALCIPPE

Oh, do I need to catalogue the rest?
"*Baldachin*'s" not enough? All right. A test.

"Flotilla." Does "flotilla" ring a bell?

CLARICE

Not really.

ALCIPPE

Maybe *"pomegranate"*?

CLARICE

          Well,
I do like pomegranates, truth to tell.

ALCIPPE

Ah-ha! I wonder you can say the word...

CLARICE

"Pomegranate"?

ALCIPPE

       ...and not turn into a curd
Of quivering, pasty shame! The word's mere sound...

CLARICE

"Pomegranate"?

ALCIPPE

       ...should fling you to the ground,
Onto your knees, and leave you there to squirm.

CLARICE

Why? Is there something lethal in the term
"Pome" — ?

ALCIPPE

Will you stop saying "pomegranate"?

CLARICE

Could you explain...

ALCIPPE

      You've taken me for granted
All too long. Who am I, your party clown?
Explain? What for? Your uncle might come down!

CLARICE

I swear...

ALCIPPE

The next time you take out your *barge,*

Could you not publicize the trip at large?

CLARICE
My barge?

ALCIPPE
      Yes, next time you decide to cheat,
Why don't you choose a lover more discreet?

CLARICE
A lover?

ALCIPPE
      Oh, he's told me everything —
With orchestra and chorus there to sing
An oratorio about your jaunt!

CLARICE
And who's this lover, please?

ALCIPPE
           Dorante.

CLARICE
                Dorante?!

ALCIPPE
Oh, yes, that's good. That's very credible.

CLARICE
Dorante?

ALCIPPE
      "Oh, *who?*" You found him beddable
Enough last night!

CLARICE
      I've never met the man!

ALCIPPE
Then why'd I see the father of his clan
Leaving your house just now with my own eyes?

CLARICE
My uncle's an old friend of his.

ALCIPPE
      Oh, lies, lies!

CLARICE

He *is!*

ALCIPPE

Is this a stage? Are these just props?
Perhaps Dorante's for nighttime, day's for Pops!

CLARICE

Alcippe, I've never even seen his face!

ALCIPPE

Was it too dim inside your trysting place?
Inside your *baldachin?* You had a date
With cherry ices, alabaster plates,
Five boats with blindfold virgins, calf, cock, pig,
Chateau Lafite, God knows what else to swig,
You spend a whole night being jocular,
You didn't spot your interlocutor?
A thousand Roman candles shoot through space
Spilling their loads of luminescent spume,
Their artificial sun banishing gloom,
And yet you somehow never glimpsed his face?
You didn't peek, you didn't drop the screen
While posing as some naked tangerine?
You didn't spy between your sprawling members?

CLARICE

Well, if I did, I think that I'd remember.

ALCIPPE

You think that I could make this up?

CLARICE

No, no...

ALCIPPE

It's fine. Run off with your Dorante. Go. Go!
Forget Alcippe, the man who loved you once.

CLARICE

I might. Now will you hear me out, you dunce?
I spent last night right here on my rear end.

ALCIPPE

Don't raise your voice. Your uncle might descend.
If he's up there. If he exists at all.

Hello! Is anybody — ?

CLARICE
Stop this brawl!
What will convince you this is some huge blunder?

ALCIPPE
The settling of our marriage, since you wonder.
Marry me tomorrow, all my doubts are spent.

CLARICE
But what about your Dad — Lord Gout of Ghent?

ALCIPPE
I'll handle him.

CLARICE
You think that he won't frown?

ALCIPPE
Clarice...

CLARICE
Stop. Wait. My uncle's coming down.
You're joking, right? Oh, pug. You're such a fool.
(CLARICE exits.)

ALCIPPE
Go. Giggle. Heap Alcippe with ridicule!
Each snigger only frees me from your rule,
Each snicker snaps another chain. Snap! Snap!
I loved Clarice. She gave me my first slap
Standing right here — no, here — on this parquet.
How many a fight have these planks underlay,
How many break-ups and make-up bouquets...
But now that nouveau fop would snap her up,
My pseudo-friend would taste her hungry kiss,
Would lick Clarice's minty dentifrice?
(Draws his sword.)
Let's see how well he likes the taste of this.
I'll spear that double-dealing troubadour!
Not here, though. I don't want to stain Our Floor.
I'll leave him nowhere to put on his cap,
I'll slice him into bits, I'll leave no scrap,
With snap! And snap! I must stop saying that.
Oh, what the hell. Snap, snap, snap, *snap!*
(ALCIPPE exits.)

Scene Three.

(The Place Royale. Clarice's house at right. Lucrece's house at left. GERONTE enters.)

GERONTE
Dorante! This lassitude is unbecoming!
My wedding plans are absolutely humming.
The Place Royale — and there's Clarice's house.
Now I need only show his future spouse
The lad and she'll corral him on the instant.

(DORANTE and CLITON enter, DORANTE studying a map.)

DORANTE
"The Place Royale. G-3..." It can't be distant,
Cliton. We're right in its vicinity.

CLITON
(Points to a street sign.)
Well, doesn't that say...

DORANTE
                    Ah, divinity!
I sense your presence in this sweet locale!
Where are you, O my darling?

CLITON
                    ..."Place Royale"?

DORANTE
If I don't find her, I shall go insane.

GERONTE
Well, well. Now isn't this a handsome lane!
What time is it, Dorante?

DORANTE
                    What? Nearly three.

GERONTE
Perfect. Why don't you step out of the lee
Into the sun. And look at these fine buildings!
The ornaments, the pediments, the gilding!
These silvery trees — it's like some pastorale!

DORANTE

Yes, very nice...
(Just notices a street sign.)
               (Cliton — the Place Royale!)

GERONTE

(Moves DORANTE forward to be better seen.)
Don't hug the walk.

DORANTE

           (Lucrece lives on this row!)

GERONTE

Chin up. Hands at your sides. Good. Shoulders low.
(A church clock chimes three o'clock.)

GERONTE

There's three o'clock!

DORANTE

          Um, Dad, are we expected?

GERONTE

My boy, you realize I've not neglected
Your welfare.

DORANTE

         No, sir. I'd say, *au contraire.*
(Behind them, CLARICE and LUCRECE appear in a window of Clarice's house. GERONTE signals to say, "This is he.")

DORANTE

Why are you waving?

GERONTE

         Waving?

DORANTE

           In the air.
(During the following, DORANTE keeps wandering away, GERONTE keeps pulling him back into position beneath the window.)

GERONTE

A muscle cramp. Well, now you'd go to war.
And given the perils that might lie in store —
I know how thirst for glory tempts young blades
To risk their necks in reckless escapades —

It seems to me you need a brake to slow you,
A rub, some inner skid, a check to show you
You needn't be too quick to waste your life.
And what could check you better than your wife?

DORANTE

My what — ?

GERONTE

    I'll get you married, and with speed.
The only thing we lack 's the wedding deed.

DORANTE

But, sir...

GERONTE

   She's beautiful. She's rich...

DORANTE

         Sublime.
But, sir, these things take thought, and talk, and time.

GERONTE

No need. Her uncle's an old friend of mine.
She lives right on this street.

DORANTE

      She what?

GERONTE

          It's true.
Indeed, *the lady has her eye on you.*

DORANTE

It couldn't *be*...

GERONTE

   Yes.

DORANTE

   Sir, I know this niece!

GERONTE

You do?

DORANTE

   We met today!

GERONTE
You know...?

DORANTE
                        Lucrece?

GERONTE
Clarice?

DORANTE
I do! What? *Who?*

GERONTE
            Clarice.

DORANTE
                        Clarice?
No, no. It's some mistake. Clarice?

GERONTE
                    The same.

DORANTE
But, father, I know no one by that name.

GERONTE
Well, you will now. She'll carry on our line.

DORANTE
No, please.

GERONTE
        I want a grandson.

DORANTE
                    Grandson? Fine.
But not by some *Clarice*. Oh, please, sir. *Please.*

GERONTE
I say you will.

DORANTE
(Clasps Geronte's legs.)
                I beg you! On my knees!

GERONTE
Get up!

DORANTE
And anyway, I can't. You see?

GERONTE
You can't?

DORANTE
Complete impossibility.

GERONTE
But why?

DORANTE
Well — inadmissibility.

GERONTE
Inadmiss... You don't mean virility?

DORANTE
No, no.

GERONTE
Sterility? Fertility?

DORANTE
I'm speaking, sir, of immorility.
Morality. And illegality.

GERONTE
Why?

DORANTE
Well, in Poitiers...

GERONTE
Say, or on my life —
Why can't you wed?

DORANTE
Because I have a wife.

GERONTE
WHAT?!

CLITON
WHAT?!

GERONTE
Without my knowledge, or consent?

DORANTE

They forced me, sir. O, curse the sad event!
If you but knew the trials I underwent.

GERONTE

Well, tell me all. *Don't weep.* But if you hide
The truth...

DORANTE

    Who, I, sir?

GERONTE

        All right, who's this bride?

DORANTE

Her family's noble, if downwardly mobile.
Her name's Orphise. Her father, Armidon.

GERONTE

I've never heard of either one. Go on.
(As DORANTE acts out the story, CLARICE and LUCRECE look on, baffled.)

DORANTE

There is a willow grows aslant a brook.
'Twas there I first beheld her, saw the look
Of gypsy in those eyes, those calves of cream
As she hised up her skirts to toe the stream.
I didn't dawdle. In an hour I knew
Her name, within a day we'd met, in two
We two'd confessed our crush, within a week
I'd vault her wall and mount a bush to seek
Her in her room and whisper, lip to lobe.
But then one night Orphise lay in her robe —
O fateful date! The second of September!
It's more than I can bear to re-remember! —
We hear a sound. A footstep in the hall.
Her father's voice outside. "Daughter!" he calls,
And pounds our door, unwisely left unlocked.
"One minute, sir!" she stalls, while I, half-cocked,
Go scrambling for the window. There's no time.
He's coming in. But she — a genius — climbs
His neck, embracing him, while I secrete
Myself behind the bed. He takes a seat
This far away from me, and starts to talk,

The Liar, adapted by David Ives from the comedy by Pierre Corneille   **35**

Showing some ring, a diamond like a rock.
But suddenly my blood begins to freeze.
Some suitor wants to wed...
(He can't remember her name.)

GERONTE
Orphise...?

DORANTE
Orphise!

I stop my mouth to stifle a mad moan.
"Say, what was that?" her father says. "That groan..."
"A fart," she says. *"Pardón."*

GERONTE
She's brilliant.

DORANTE
Right?

But now the blanket's fallen. I'm in sight!
So casually she covers me with bedding,
Placates her Dad about this cursèd wedding.
He's slinking out now with his vulgar ring
When suddenly...
(A pause. He's at a loss.)

GERONTE
Well, what?

DORANTE
"Ding ding ding ding!"

My watch goes off!

GERONTE & CLITON
No!

DORANTE
Yes! "Now what's that noise?"

He cries. "My watch," says she, completely poised.
Suspicion burns within his beady eyes.
"What watch? From where? Some cad? I'll have no lies!
I swear to God I'll scatter this man's brains!
Show me the thing!" "Yes, father." She maintains
Her cool and turns to me and winks, I grab the fob,
When suddenly the...

GERONTE

What?

DORANTE

The... thingmabob...

GERONTE

The watch?

DORANTE

No.

CLITON

Stem?

DORANTE

Oh, what d'you call it...?

GERONTE

Chain?

DORANTE

Yes! Catches on my pistol's trigger. *Bang!*
The girl falls headlong.

GERONTE

Dead?

DORANTE

Apparently.
I spring to view. Her Dad, transparently
Terrified, runs into the hall and yells
"Assassin! Murder!" Voices are heard. Bells
Outside. With Tarquin's ravishing stride I
Attempt the hall. There's no place to hide. I
See servants bounding up the stairs. I draw
My knife, but — *damn!* — it shatters in my claw,
Struck by a bullet! Flinging off the pieces
I back into the room. Meanwhile, Orphise's
Crise — nothing but a fainting spell — has passed.
We seize some furniture and, working fast,
Erect a barricade against the door.
The mattress, dresser, wardrobe, junk galore,
The chamber pot, the trunks —

GERONTE

All right, all right!

DORANTE

We seem to've sealed ourselves in nice and tight,
We've just embraced into a seamless ball...

GERONTE

Yes? Suddenly — ?

DORANTE

A battering ram bursts through the wall.

GERONTE & CLITON

No!

DORANTE

Yes! We're almost buried under plaster!
And then comes striding through the hole... The Master!

GERONTE

Her father.

DORANTE

Yes. Um...

GERONTE

Armid...

DORANTE

Armidon!
And so I did what any man had done.

GERONTE

You wed.

DORANTE

I dead. I did. And so, dear father,
I won a prize with just a spot of bother
That Jupiter would give Olympus for.
Condemn me. Call me simple. I adore!
(CLARICE and LUCRECE leave the window.)

GERONTE

No, no. I won't play God. I'm not a stone.
Whom love hath joined are soldered at the bone.

DORANTE

How true, how true.

GERONTE

But why so mum, dear boy?
You wouldn't share your news with me? Your joy?

DORANTE

I only feared her dowry'd be too meager.

GERONTE

What need for dowry? You're on fire. She's eager.
True love's a pearl, mere property....

DORANTE

A carbuncle.

GERONTE

I'm going to settle with Clarice's uncle
And call that wedding off.
(Embracing him.)

Congratulations!

DORANTE

Thanks, Dad.
(GERONTE exits.)

So how'd you like my latest fabulation?

CLITON

Your what?

DORANTE

My shpiel.

CLITON

You mean that wedding wasn't *real*?

DORANTE

A stratagem to shed this foul Clarice
And gently substitute the fair Lucrece.

CLITON

Yeah, but...

DORANTE

Imagine if I hadn't lied!
I'd be engaged right now *to the wrong bride!*
You see, you need a lie with proper flavor...

CLITON

Monsieur...

DORANTE

Cliton?

CLITON

Could you do me a favor?
Next time you're lying, could you, like, shoot a wink?
A poke, a wave, a nod — or whatever you think —
So while you're fictifying in full spectrum
I don't just stand there like some gaping rectum?

DORANTE

Fear not, my friend. To show I comprehend,
I hereby name you my sole confidante.
My second soul. The conscience of Dorante.
Depository of my inmost key,
And closest nursemaid of my bosom.

CLITON

Gee.
That's somewhat closer than I planned to be.

DORANTE

And no more lies. I swear. Today I cease.
(SABINE enters with a letter, looking around.)

DORANTE

Good *God!*

CLITON

What, what?

DORANTE

The servant of Lucrece!
Speak to me, maiden! Ask me what you want!

SABINE

I'm looking for some rascal named "Dorante"?

DORANTE

That's me!
(DORANTE grabs the letter and steps aside to read it.)

CLITON

Hello, there. You?

SABINE

I beg your pardon?

CLITON

We meet again.

SABINE

We do?

CLITON

The Twillery garden?

Today? The trees?

SABINE

I've never seen you in my life.

CLITON

The grass? The breeze? A conversation rife
With innuendo?

SABINE

I don't think so.

CLITON

What's this? *Tact?*

SABINE

Please go away.

CLITON

Okay. Okay. React
Like that. I was an asshole.

SABINE

Really!

CLITON

Wait!
All that I said about you being an eight — ?
It's just I have this problem with the truth.
I have to say it all the time!

SABINE

Forsooth.

CLITON

Just watch. I'll try to tell you you're a ten.
You're a t... You're a t... I'll try a pen.
("Writes" on his hand.)
You're a t... You're a t...

SABINE
This is inane.

CLITON
Now where's that room key?
(She slaps him.)
                    What are you, *insane?*

DORANTE
Ha, ha! Here's my reply: I'd be delighted.
(SABINE exits.)
                                    God!
Doubt on, Cliton! You poor benighted sod.

CLITON
Who, me? Just now I was your bosom's nurse!

DORANTE
A tender invitation interspersed
With delicate endearments. Look. "*Adonis.*"
That's me.

CLITON
                    What is she, blind?

DORANTE
                                    Perceptive. Honest.
"Please meet me for a late-night tête-a-tête."
The girl I met this morning. Want to bet?
But I need information, facts to go on.
Lucrece's family, history and so on.
I want it all in here...
(Points to his head.)
                                    ... as I require.
Memory! Keystone of the master liar!
So ask around. Go weasel out her dāta.

CLITON
Just keep that crazy maid away. Well — later!
(CLITON exits.)

DORANTE
Lucrezia! Italian might allure her...
"*Che bella notte...! Che bella figura...!*"
(PHILISTE enters, bows formally.)

PHILISTE

Monsieur.
(Holds out a note.)
              Alcippe awaits you in the Bois.

DORANTE

What's this? Another note for poor old moi?
I certainly am popular today.
"Thou bastard. Meet me, bring a sword — and pray."
And what offense could force my childhood neighbor
To make me spit him on my trusty sabre?

PHILISTE

The rules of honor, section 40, say
A challenge mayn't be questioned, come what may.

DORANTE

Ah, yes, old section 40, I'd forgot.
Well, tell him I'll be there. To die — or not.
(More bows. PHILISTE exits.)
O, Paris, how I love you! Geez, it's fast here.
At this rate I don't see how I can last here.
I just arrived, I haven't any pull,
And look — my calendar's already full!
Fess up. Are any of you as quick as I —
The master of the airtight alibi?
As sly, yet trusty on the witness stand?
A certain Senator just raised his hand.
I'm sorry, sir. No chance. I win the laurel.
First challenge? Right. Alcippe's mysterious quarrel.
Well, it's a chance for exercise, some sun.
Let's see how I finesse it. Might be fun.
(Exits, whistling.)

Scene Four.

(The Bois de Boulogne. ALCIPPE and PHILISTE enter.)

PHILISTE
(Entering:)
No, no, no no...

ALCIPPE
My pride and honor are at stake, Philiste.

PHILISTE
You lose both, fighting with this arriviste.
And all for what? I swear — a misperception.

ALCIPPE
Upon my oath, he'll die for this deception.
Enough!
(DORANTE enters.)

DORANTE
Well, gentlemen.

ALCIPPE
You got my note?

DORANTE
I must have, since I'm here. So. Shall we smote?

PHILISTE
Gentlemen, might I make one last appeal?

ALCIPPE
Too late. The gauntlet's thrown, there's no repeal.

PHILISTE
Then take your marks. Who first draws blood is victor.

DORANTE
Who first draws blood...?

PHILISTE
Or kills.

DORANTE
Ah, good. Much stricter.
(ALCIPPE and DORANTE take their places with hands on their hilts.)

PHILISTE

En garde!
(DORANTE is instantly in motion, only miming drawing his sword,
just as he mimes all the following. ALCIPPE and PHILISTE merely
stare, boggled.)

DORANTE

       And *ding!* They're off! Dorante is quick
Out of his corner, with an expert *flick*
He plunges in the fray! Left lunge! Right jab!
My God, this kid can play! *Another* stab,
And yet another! Wow! He nips the sleeve
Of his opponent!
(ALCIPPE grabs his sleeve as if hit.)
               Now the other sleeve!
(ALCIPPE grabs the other sleeve.)
There's still no blood. Alcippe looks stunned! He stands
There in a daze while Kid Dorante just dances
Rings around him! He's backing off... Alcippe's
Retreating now... Is this the end? Is he
Conceding? Is Alcippe just going to lay low?
But wait! Alcippe's in action now!
(ALCIPPE, too, mimes drawing his sword.)
                  The halo
Is off, the gloves are on! *Alcippe* attacks!
And *one*, he goes out left! And *two*, he shags
Off right! Dorante ripostes... ripostes again...
And now they both go at it with a yen!
Their blades so quick they might as well be air!
And parry, lunge, and look! With savoir faire
Each snips a lock of his opponent's hair!
(Each grabs at his hair to check.)
Oh, what a duel, ladies and gentlemen,
What a duel! Three rounds in and no blood spilt!
But wait! What's this? They're chest to chest! They're hilt
To hilt!
(The two press chests, eye to eye.)
        These kids are close enough to floss!
Who'll crack? Who'll flinch? Who'll give the *coop da grace*?
Who'll be horizontal when he leaves this ring?
Is this *ka-ching* for one of these fine —

PHILISTE

DING!

I mean, all hold!
(ALCIPPE and DORANTE part.)
Both gentlemen have honored Honor's law,
Therefore I deem this duel a noble draw.

DORANTE

Fine. Chalk this match love-love. But for the audit
I'd love to know the reason that we fought it.
Has someone slandered me?
(Pulls an imaginary pistol.)

I'll shoot the chough!

ALCIPPE

You ought to know the reason well enough.

PHILISTE

Tell him, Alicippe. You've fought now. Call his bluff.

ALCIPPE

I'll only say two words. First: *Pomegranate*.

DORANTE

Keep going.

ALCIPPE

Baldachin. You didn't plan it
As an affront, your intimate excursion
In some giant punt, then describing this diversion
Down to a certain naked tangerine?
You didn't know, you stinking libertine,
That I've been secretly engaged, betrothed
To that same feral fruit whom you unclothed
With Roman candles spilling their hot sap?
Well, I say *snap*, my friend. Snap, snap, snap, snap!

DORANTE

Alcippe, you've snagged yourself in your own trap.
My sailing pal can't be your fiancée.

ALCIPPE

Why not?

DORANTE

She *has* a husband — in Calais.

Fifi's a well-fixed Florentine from Aix
Who visits me for nights of frenzied sex
Whenever she's in Paris on a "shopping trip."

ALCIPPE
Fifi...?

DORANTE
      A purple birthmark on her hip,
Red hair to here. Your girlfriend has the same?

ALCIPPE
Fifi...?

DORANTE
      So Fifi's not your girlfriend's name?

ALCIPPE
But my valet's report...

DORANTE
      Not to debunk it,
He must've mixed mine with some other junket,
Some other amatory marathon.

ALCIPPE
How could I doubt you? O, you paragon!

DORANTE
I'll say but this: beware of jealousy,
My friend. It is the green-eyed monster which
Doth mock the meat it feeds upon!

ALCIPPE
So young, and yet so wise?

DORANTE
      So young, but true.

ALCIPPE
O why can't I be wise, Dorante, like you?

DORANTE
Perhaps with time and more experience.
Adieu.
(DORANTE exits. ALCIPPE lets out a cry of frustration.)

PHILISTE

Still growling? Why?

ALCIPPE

Siberians

Don't live in deeper dark than I, Philiste!
If not Dorante, then what philandering beast
Took her in his bark? Whom did my man spy?

PHILISTE

You want to know? I'll tell you. It was I.
(ALCIPPE goes for his throat.)
But, but, but, *but!* The girl was not Clarice.
It was Sabine, wearing her ermine piece.
You know Clarice's ermine cape?

ALCIPPE

It's hooded.

PHILISTE

You know the lane at her back door?

ALCIPPE

It's wooded.

PHILISTE

The woman whom your man saw slip outside
Was not your own but my prospective bride.

ALCIPPE

You mean...?

PHILISTE

It was Sabine. So have no fear.

ALCIPPE

Sabine...?

PHILISTE

Whom I've been courting for a year.

ALCIPPE

You mean...?

PHILISTE

A servant, hence the need for stealth.

ALCIPPE

Sabine...?!

PHILISTE
Whom I, in spite of all my wealth,
My taste, my style, my elegant chateau
Am nuts for. And whom I, in my bateau,
Took for a quiet row along the river,
With one guitar — no band — and chicken liver.
I tried to set you straight about my outing.
You wouldn't hear.

ALCIPPE
No, I was busy shouting.
Sabine? No.

PHILISTE
Yes!

ALCIPPE
That scourge?

PHILISTE
So call it sickness.
I love the girl, Alcippe. I love her strictness.
She's adamant as truth, she's hard to rattle,
And on a picnic — expert with a paddle.

ALCIPPE
Then I shall love her, too! Platonically.
But wait. You mean this duel...?

PHILISTE
Ironically,
Was over nothing. Oh, and by the by?
All that about his mistress was a lie.

ALCIPPE
There's no libidinous creature from Aix?

PHILISTE
A feature of his inner multiplex.

ALCIPPE
No well-fixed Florentine?

PHILISTE
He traded up.

ALCIPPE
No luminescent spume?

PHILISTE
He made it up.
Did anyone in town see a scintilla?
Or hear an orchestra?

ALCIPPE
So no flotilla?

PHILISTE
No calf.

ALCIPPE
No cock?

PHILISTE
No figs on the buffet.
How could there be? He just arrived today!

ALCIPPE
He minted all those lies? I stand in awe.

PHILISTE
Well, don't forget, Alcippe: he studied law.

ALCIPPE
What shall we do?

PHILISTE
With him? I hereby prophesy:
Dorante will get his just desserts. Just let him lie.
(They exit.)

Scene Five.

(Clarice's bedroom. Evening. CLARICE, LUCRECE and SABINE. CLARICE is getting dressed.)

CLARICE
Can you imagine? — Lace me up, Sabine. —
Dorante — on whom this father was so keen —
Turns out to be none other than the dear
But daffy musketeer who bent my ear
And my poor hand this morning on the green!

LUCRECE
"Poor hand"? You almost made a gift of it.

CLARICE
Sometimes one does things for the lift of it.
At least he promises a lively time.

LUCRECE
You mean his gift for antic pantomime?

CLARICE
Yes, what was that?

LUCRECE
                          His complicated dance?
His brief compendium of French romance
With every plot twist, minus all the patter?

CLARICE
I couldn't hear the words.

LUCRECE
                          But would it matter?

CLARICE
So he's Dorante! Who knows? This might be fate.

LUCRECE
That's what girls often say — *before* the date.
(SABINE finishes fastening Clarice's dress, and exits.)

CLARICE
Oh, poor, untried Lucrece.

LUCRECE
                          You think *I'm* green?

When *you* think he's a soldier?

CLARICE
                    What — you mean...?

LUCRECE
Your so-called "musketeer"? Oh, poor Clarice.
This guy's so slippery he's a sea of grease.
Men cook up battles, conjure naval storms —
They know how maidens melt at uniforms,
And then to please some girl their brain begot,
Impersonate a person whom they're not.
This one's quite dear. A diamond in the raw.
He's probably a student. I'd say Law.
He'd lie to anyone, be it him, be it her...

CLARICE
How did you *learn* all this?

LUCRECE
                    By going to the theatre.

CLARICE
Well, as a trickster he out-tops the heap.
He duped not only me. He duped Alcippe.
Something about a baldachin, a boat —
Enough to make my sweetie bark and gloat.
"Pomegranate! Pomegranate!" he kept shouting,
Apparently the highlight of this outing —
Except the fireworks' pornographic spume
That found me sprawling naked, as the gloom
Was brightened by their artificial sun.
Now that I think of it, it sounds like fun.

LUCRECE
But this must mean Dorante's in love with you...!
Today when he was hand in glove with you
His heart, however slippery, must have seen
That you're predestined as his lifelong queen.
Wedding his native cleverness to Fate,
Undoubtedly aware Alcippe's your mate —
Intended mate, at any rate — and zealous
To win, he tricked Alcippe to make him jealous
With all those baldachins and blindfold virgins.
Then! Working brilliantly as any surgeon,

He sent his father here to intercede,
To claim your hand and frame a wedding deed,
Leaving Alcippe abandoned in the haze!

CLARICE

Lucrece, I think you've seen too many plays.
He's no Leander. I'm no Hellespont.
(SABINE enters with a letter.)

SABINE

A message, madam, from Monsieur Geronte.

LUCRECE

You don't believe me? Skeptic! Why d'you scoff?

CLARICE

(Reads the letter.)
Well, this is interesting. The wedding's off.

LUCRECE

What? With Dorante? Why?

CLARICE

                    My theories are rife.

SABINE

I'll tell you why: the young man *has* a wife.

CLARICE & LUCRECE

NO!!

SABINE

      Yes. I overheard his father say
Dorante has wed a gypsy from Poitiers.

LUCRECE

He *can't* be married! How could he have sought you?

CLARICE

I guess that's one thing theatre never taught you.
A wedded gander too will have his geese.
Well, now it's time for me to play Lucrece.

LUCRECE

But if he's married, why still keep this tryst?

CLARICE

To watch him squirm and dodge, and make him twist.

Sabine, please post your sister at the gate.
We'll serve this trickster on an alabaster plate.
(All exit.)

Scene Six.

(The garden gate at Lucrece's house. Night. DORANTE and CLITON enter.)

DORANTE

This must be it — and isn't this ironic?
We're off the Place Royale!

CLITON

        Wow, man. *Harmonic.*
(Takes out paper.)
I got that private info on Lucrece.
Her Dad's a hotshot judge. Her Mom's deceased...

DORANTE

Her father's name?

CLITON

        Perander. Rich as God.
A Tuscan villa. Ski place in Gstaad...

DORANTE

Perander. Tuscany.
(Points to head.)
        It's there. Entire.
Memory! Keystone of the master liar!

CLITON

I wish she had your tricky disposition,
To even out this evening's competition.
If she was born to lie, I'd be elated.

DORANTE

Liars aren't born, Cliton. They're fabricated.
(Across the gate, ISABELLE, CLARICE and LUCRECE enter.)

ISABELLE

(It's he.)

CLARICE

   (It's he.)

DORANTE

   (It's she. Watch this.)

CLARICE

        (The fool.)

DORANTE
Lucrece?

CLARICE
Dorante?

DORANTE
'Tis I, madame. Your willing tool.
Lay down your law. Subject me to your rule!

LUCRECE
(You recognize the style? Torrid, but florid?)

CLARICE
(But has he recognized my voice? It's horrid.)

CLITON
(It's her, okay. I recognize the voice.)

DORANTE
(What did I say? And you still doubted me?)

CLARICE
(I hope to God I haven't outed me.)

DORANTE
Sweet Aphrodite!

CLITON
(Me?)

DORANTE
(Her.)
Would I could efface
The years I've spent not living in your grace.
To live without you's fate's most cruel blow.
It's hardly life at all. It's death, it's woe.
Make me your slave, your pawn, your dog, your pet!

CLARICE
(Strong words for someone whom he's never met.
Lucrece, what did you put into that note?)

LUCRECE
(This speech is prerehearsed. It's one long quote.)

DORANTE
You are to me as thread is to the eyelet,

As the well-rounded rhyme is to the triolet,
As key to lock, as rain is to the —

CLITON
(Toilet.)

DORANTE
— violet.
You put to shame the paradise that's Dante's!
You are a peak atop the highest —

CLITON
(Panties.)

DORANTE
— Andes!
(DORANTE silently remonstrates with CLITON, while...)

CLARICE
(You go to plays. What do I say to *that*?)

LUCRECE
(It might be best to lower the thermostat.
Express some cautious interest. Toy with him.)

CLARICE
(Just what does "cautious" mean?)

LUCRECE
(Be coy with him.
Be distant. Play the comic ingénue.)

CLARICE
(Distant and cautious.)

LUCRECE
(Ape me. I'll be you.
My God, you're sexy!)

CLARICE
God, you're sex... (That's *cautious*?)

LUCRECE
(You want to make him twist?)

CLARICE
(I want to make him nauseous.
I want his head turned back-to-front and spinning,

But not with compliments.)

LUCRECE
(Clarice, you're winning.

He's in your power.)

DORANTE
Did I hear you say "sexy,"

My dove?

LUCRECE
(Indeed.)

CLARICE
Indeed.

LUCRECE
(Like apoplexy...)

CLARICE
Like apoplexy...

LUCRECE
(You make boil my blood.)

CLARICE
You make... (No, really?) ... you make boil my blood?

LUCRECE
(I am a torrent.)

CLARICE
I am a torrent.

LUCRECE
(A flood!)

CLARICE
A flood!

LUCRECE
(Come find me, god!)

CLARICE
Come find me, god???

LUCRECE
(I am a spring! Thou'rt my divining rod!)

CLARICE

(I won't say that.)

LUCRECE

(You *must*.)

CLARICE

(*Divining rod?*)

DORANTE

(This girl is deep.)

CLITON

(So deep she's got two voices.)

DORANTE

Sweet lady, how my listening heart rejoices!
You cherish me. I'll serve you without cease.
I kneel to say it. Marry me, Lucrece!

CLARICE

You mean Clarice.

LUCRECE

You mean Lucrece!

CLARICE

Lucrece!

CLITON

(You didn't hear that? Christ, she's like a chorus!)

DORANTE

(It's *love*. They get that way, get more sonorous.)

CLARICE

My broken voice should help you to infer
The shock of your proposal. For, good sir,
Your suit is impish and impossible.

DORANTE

For you? The wildest river's crossible,
The vortex of Charybdis a mere eddy!

CLARICE

But can you wed me when you're wed already?

DORANTE

What? Who? I? Married? That's a slanderous libel!

A calumny! I'd swear it on a Bible!
May God erase me if I have a spouse!

CLITON
(Hey, watch your step.)

DORANTE
(It's true!)

CLARICE
(He's such a louse.)

DORANTE
Mademoiselle, teach me. How can I persuade you?

CLARICE
What need? Your gypsy marriage has unmade you.

DORANTE
I know: meet me at dawn at altarside.
All doubts will be undone when you're my bride.

CLARICE
Bigamist! You don't fear you'd be unmasked
By all those other women whom you've asked?

DORANTE
I only fear the jealousies I'd stir,
The thousand envious duels that I'd incur.

CLARICE
What? *You* fear duels? With all the wars you've won?

DORANTE
You know how many men I've killed?

CLARICE
Yes. *None.*

DORANTE
But crimson streams...

CLARICE
The only "crimson streams"
You've spilled were in your cups — or in your dreams.
You must have magic powers, though, I must say.
You've been in Paris six months, is that right?
Yet physically you just arrived *last night*?

DORANTE

Uhhh...

CLARICE

What, no words? What is this sudden shyness?

DORANTE

Uhhh...

CLARICE

Tell me, how was breakfast with *Her Highness?*

DORANTE

Uhhh....

CLARICE

Well, well. Tongue-tied, sir? The facts must scare you.

CLITON

(Finiggle outa this one, sir. I dare you.)

CLARICE

As for your nuptials —

DORANTE

Darling, they were feigned!
Your admiration will be unrestrained
When you hear *why* I feigned them.

CLARICE

Mere caprice?

DORANTE

My goal was simple. To win you, Lucrece.
I had to fake that marriage to undo
A union that my father had in view.

CLARICE

(This should be good. Here comes some epic saga.)

DORANTE

Some dowager, "Clarice." I'm sure she's gaga.
I? Wed some shrew? Obscene, oblong, obese?
And not the fair, the fine, divine Lucrece?

CLARICE

I know Clarice quite well, just to be fair.
Indeed, Clarice goes with me everywhere.

CLITON
(She knows Clarice?)

DORANTE
(Well, isn't that ironic.
Clarice must be her friend, the catatonic.)

CLARICE
You have strong feelings, sir.

DORANTE
One does get finical
When threatened with Clarice the Clinical.
O, be my bride!

CLARICE
Such ardor makes me wary.
Not knowing me, why would you want to marry?

DORANTE
Not knowing you? (The thing!)
(Motions hastily for the paper. CLITON digs for it.)

CLARICE
Not that I doubt you.

DORANTE
My dear Lucrece, why, I know all about you!
(Squints at the paper, trying to read.)
Your brother's dead.

CLITON
(Her *mother.*)

DORANTE
Mother's dead.
Your father's hot... fudge?

CLITON
(*Judge.*)

DORANTE
Just as I said,
A judge. His name is Derrr...

CLITON
(Peran...)

DORANTE

Deran...

CLITON

(*Peran...*)

DORANTE

Perander. The son of a kook.

CLITON

(A *duke.*)

DORANTE

Estruscan...

CLITON

(*Tuscan.*)

DORANTE

Shire, spire...

CLITON

(Squire.)

DORANTE

Squire.

A ski chalet. What more do you require?

CLITON

(Memory! Keystone of the master liar!)

DORANTE

And you say I don't know you? Ask away!

CLARICE

(I think he wants you, cuz.)

LUCRECE

(Or my chalet.)

CLARICE

But this Clarice of yours. Obese, obscene?
Some find her quite the glamorous gamine.

DORANTE

There's only one thing missing from the tart.
A personality. A ticking heart.

CLARICE
A friend of yours proposed to her this afternoon.

DORANTE
Good luck. I'd rather wed a dead baboon.

CLITON
(*Nice one.*)

CLARICE
Yet just this morning you were seen with her,
Fondling her paw, oblivious of her fur.

DORANTE
Another lie! The paw, the fur — well, both!

LUCRECE
(I don't believe it!)

CLARICE
(Watch — another oath.)

DORANTE
Lucrece, I swear!

CLARICE & LUCRECE
(Ten points.)

DORANTE
                            As God is true,
The only girl I've met today is you!

CLARICE
Well, that's enough! The impudence! The gall!
I didn't see you two myself, eyeball
To eyeball? How pathetic, how transparent!
Even when forced to face the facts you daren't!
You lie, you swear, and sully what you swore!
You breathe deceit, you skunk, from every pore.
Find an asbestos tux and button it well
Because I'll only marry you *in hell!*
You dog, you beast, you cad, you... son of a bitch!
(*CLARICE and LUCRECE exit.*)

CLITON
Well, I'd say that went off without a hitch.
Was all that "kiss me," in some private code?

Say "Germany" and watch — she will *explode*.

DORANTE
Cliton, I'm this close.

CLITON
Close to what?

DORANTE
To winning!

CLITON
What, her? This was the end of the last inning!
You lost! She called you *liar*!

DORANTE
I don't know why.

CLITON
Well, maybe 'cause you had your pants on fire!

DORANTE
But everything I said to her was true!

CLITON
Encyclopedias turn to lies with guys like you.

DORANTE
Did I say she was deep? This girl's an ocean!

CLITON
So that explains this weird bi-polar motion?

DORANTE
She's playing hard to get. Fine. What a day!

CLITON
What are you gonna do?

DORANTE
A soft duvet
And six hours' dreaming ought to show the way.
Let me submit my mind unto the moon —
Lucrece will be my wife by afternoon.
Good night, Cliton. Sweet dreams.
(DORANTE exit.)

CLITON
This guy's a loon!

(ISABELLE pokes her head through the gate.)

ISABELLE

Hello there.

CLITON

   Ahhhh!

ISABELLE

   Remember me? It's Izzy.

CLITON

You recognize me?

ISABELLE

   What?

CLITON

   I'm getting dizzy

In my old age, I guess.

ISABELLE

   Could I forget you?

CLITON

        Yes.

You did before.

ISABELLE

   I came to let you know the score.
Just tell your master he should keep on hoping.

CLITON

After all *that?* He's lucky he's still coping.

ISABELLE

Lucrece — I mean the *real* Lucrece? — let's say...
She finds him *very interesting.*

CLITON

   Oh-kay.

(Aside:)
What "real Lucrece"? Guess she's a duet.
Part one's the wacko harpy we just met.

LUCRECE

(Offstage:)
Isabelle!

ISABELLE

You're so cute.

(She kisses him.)

                                 Au revoir, my swell.

(She kisses him and exits.)

CLITON

I too submit me to the moon! Ah, Isabelle,
Sweet Isabelle, who really truly is a belle!
I'd find more rhymes if only she were visabelle.
Is it not risibelle how most invisabelle
The indivisibelle Isabelle... is?
And oh, how miserabelle am I, bereft of peace.
But hey, what's this about "the real Lucrece"?
And after that he shouldn't give up hope?

(SABINE enters from Clarice's house.)

SABINE

Hey! You!

CLITON

             Ah, there you are, my canteloupe!

(She slaps him.)

Say, what was *that?*

SABINE

             I'll give you both what-for.

CLITON

What *for?*

SABINE

             For being on this street. Now scat!

(SABINE exits.)

CLITON

The maid is just as schizo as her matron.
Well, what a day, to quote my crazy patron.
So that's Act One. Think I'll go have a think.

(SABINE sticks her head out.)

SABINE

Hey! *Hey!*

CLITON

           I'm going!

(To us:)

And you — go have a drink!

(CLITON exits.)

END OF ACT ONE

(The Place Royale. Morning. DORANTE enters. CLITON drags in behind him.)

DORANTE

Still barely dawn. She draws me like a lure.
And here's her street! My dreams in miniature!
Lucrece, my love! Lucrece!

CLITON

                Monsieur Dorante?
It isn't *dawn* yet for a debutante.
The rich live in their whole own later time zone,
So quit your shouting or we'll be a crime zone.

DORANTE

Let them arrest me, throw the book at me!
I must get her this note.
(Produces a letter.)

CLITON

            Don't look at me.

DORANTE

My brain's on fire, Cliton, and she's the fuel.

CLITON

What's this I hear — Alcippe, he fought some duel?

DORANTE

Alcippe?

CLITON

        Your friend?

DORANTE

        A duel?

CLITON

            Uh-huh.

DORANTE

             With whom?

CLITON

Well, oddly, someone very much like you'm.

And since I was away an hour or two'm
Yesterday afternoo'm,
Would you have any info on this rumor?

DORANTE
You want the truth?

CLITON
Like any wise consumer.

DORANTE
I swore I'd not make known the sad event.
But how can any earthly vow prevent
Divulging it to you, my confidante,
My second soul, the conscience of Dorante,
Depository of my inmost key,
The closest nursemaid of my bosom?

CLITON
Gee.

So you were saying...

DORANTE
This duel.

CLITON
And your own role?

DORANTE
It is the cause, it is the cause, my soul!
For ten long years he'd stalked and baited me.
I needn't tell you why he hated me.
It was a night at cards in Paraguay.
A girl named Peepa, too much bootleg rye...
We knew that one would die at our next meeting.
You saw him yesterday. His hearty greeting
Dissembling all the venom he showed later.
He sent a challenge through an arbitrator,
We met, we fought with dagger, sword and cape.
My rapier left a gaping hole, the shape
Of Peepa's head. He fell, cold to the touch.

CLITON
No!

DORANTE

Yes.

CLITON

He's dead?

DORANTE

I left him there for such,
Face down in gore.

CLITON

Poor guy.

DORANTE

So young.

CLITON

What's more?

A gentleman. With *character.*

DORANTE

Times ten.

CLITON

Hot-headed, yeah. But *genuine?*

DORANTE

Amen.

CLITON

I doubt this world will see his like again.
(ALCIPPE enters, carrying a bottle of champagne.)

ALCIPPE

My friend! Let me embrace you! What a morning!
A miracle! Completely without warning!
I feel alive again! I could combust!

CLITON

(I have to say, your victim looks robust.)

ALCIPPE

My father's come to Paris! That old sneak.
Who would've dreamed?

CLITON

I'm dreaming as you speak.

DORANTE

I'd love to share your glee — and to augment it...

ALCIPPE

But you don't know what's up! I seem demented.
A wedding contract's in my Dad's valise.
That means I can get married to Clarice!

DORANTE

Clarice?

CLITON

Clarice?

ALCIPPE

My fiancée!

DORANTE

You jest.

ALCIPPE

I swear to God.

DORANTE

I never would've guessed.
Well, what a turn.

ALCIPPE

That's why I'm off my head!

CLITON

(I thought it was because he wasn't dead.)

ALCIPPE

I'm off to her, to get her uncle's nod.
If he exists! At this point, nothing's odd!
Then she and I can pop this sparkling wine.
I wanted you to know, for auld lang syne.
(They do their special handshake.)

DORANTE

How wonderful to know our friendship's mended.
And please, pass on my best to your intended.

ALCIPPE

I will! But now...

DORANTE
Yes, go! Go see your bride.
May Jupiter be always at your side!

ALCIPPE
Au revoir!

DORANTE
Your joy, an ever-gushing font!
(ALCIPPE exits.)

CLITON
What was I, now? Oh, yeah. Your *confidante?*
Your second soul? The conscience of Dorante?
Depository of your inmost key?
The closest nursemaid of your bosom?

DORANTE
                        Gee.
How good to see him stand there as he did.

CLITON
You mean the imaginary invalid?

DORANTE
What...? *What?* You think that I trumped up that duel?

CLITON
No disrespect. Is there a molecule
Of truth in anything that stems from there?
(Points to Dorante's mouth.)
'Cuz you lie anytime and anywhere
And prob'ly in your sleep! You can't speak truth
To Christians, Hindus, Musselmans, or Jewth!

DORANTE
I see. You were surprised to see Alcippe.

CLITON
Well, *yeah.*

DORANTE
Surprised at his recovery.

CLITON
A *bit.*

DORANTE
Well, there's this new discovery —
Perhaps you've heard of it — called "Powdered Health"?

CLITON
I've seen it on the shelf...

DORANTE
                    And what a wealth
Of healing herbs and rare ingredients.
Can't beat the stuff for sheer expedience.

CLITON
I never heard it raised you from *the dead!*
Or plugged up sword wounds shaped like some broad's head!
He woulda danced, if we'd'a had a band!

DORANTE
What you're referring to's the *regular* brand.
Cliton, through certain friends, by luck and stealth,
I have some *Extra-Strength* Brand Powdered Health.

CLITON
And it fights *death*?

DORANTE
                    I've seen men in their shroud
Leap from their coffins, blinking but unbowed.
A bachelor friend — beheaded, dead, and buried?
One dash of Extra Strength — last week he married.
Own it, you own the elixir of the ages!

CLITON
I'll give you anything. A whole year's wages.
One bottle. Just a pinch. I need it! Please!

DORANTE
The problem is, the label's in Chinese.
The hidden powers are non-Chinese resistant.
How's yours?

CLITON
                    What, my Chinese? It's non-existent!

DORANTE
Without Chinese the *jing-jong* don't react.

CLITON

You speak Chinese?

DORANTE
                    Quite fluently, in fact.
I speak ten tongues. Kashmiri, Syriac,
Algonquin, Hebrew, High Bulgarian,
Pampango, Polish, Rastafarian,
And Volapük. Not always flawless syntax...

CLITON

Jing-jong...?

DORANTE

Jing-jong.

CLITON

You need ten tongues, an onion, and an axe,
The way that you make mincemeat of the facts,
Then dish them out to folks like Truth Tartare.

DORANTE

O ye of little faith.
(GERONTE enters.)

GERONTE
                    Ah, there you are!

DORANTE

(Oh, God, not now.)

GERONTE
                    Dorante, I've had a thought.

DORANTE

(Eesh.)

GERONTE
            Given the sacredness of that close knot
That we call marriage, and the holy thunder
Of those old words, "Let no man..."

DORANTE
                                "...put asunder,"
Etcetera, yes.

GERONTE
            And given my time of life,

I have a great desire to meet your wife.
(Behind them, LUCRECE and ISABELLE show up in Lucrece's window and watch the following in puzzlement.)

DORANTE
My wife...? Oh, yes, my wife.

GERONTE
     Are you attending?
(Takes out letter.)
I've penned this to her father, recommending...
Where is it... Yes. The point of this whole letter,
That she come here, and you yourself go get her.

DORANTE
Who? *I?*

GERONTE
   Who else? It hardly warrants mention.
To send this blackguard would seem condescension.

DORANTE
Well, he'd appreciate your politesse.
Too bad her Dad would never acquiesce.

GERONTE
Not acquiesce...?

DORANTE
   I know he'd be beguiled.
But bring her *here?*

GERONTE
   And you'd be reconciled.

DORANTE
I'd love to go. I'm *dying* to go. I'm wild.

GERONTE
Then why not leave forthwith?

DORANTE
     My wife's with child.

GERONTE & CLITON
No!

DORANTE
Yes! She's six months gone. No, thirty weeks.

GERONTE
My boy! What news! O, let me kiss those cheeks!
I'm floored! A grandfather...?

DORANTE
You.

GERONTE
I'm delirious!

DORANTE
But there are complications, some quite serious...

GERONTE
No, no, I wouldn't think of tempting fate.
I've bided this long. I'm content to wait.
O heaven, you heard an old man's imprecation!
I'd wait a year!

DORANTE
(That was the implication.)

GERONTE
Farewell. I'm going to pen a second note.
(Capers.)
Unless I die of joy!

DORANTE
(Check out the old goat.)

GERONTE
I'll send congratulations and my best
To him and to the mother, counsel rest...
You too must pen a note.

DORANTE
A long one. Roger.

GERONTE
Au revoir!

DORANTE
Au revoir!
(GERONTE exits.)
You really have to love this codger,

With "imprecations" and his "notes to pen."

CLITON
Watch out, the codger's coming back again.
(GERONTE re-enters.)

GERONTE
I can't recall your in-law's name.

DORANTE
(Not a clue.)
His name...?

GERONTE
To put here on the envelope.

DORANTE
You frame
The note you want. I'll add his name and seal it.

GERONTE
Two hands might seem insulting. You don't feel it...?

DORANTE
The sentiment's what counts. He'll need a hanky.

GERONTE
Provincial gentry can be rather cranky.

DORANTE
He's very nonchalant.

GERONTE
Enough, Dorante.
What name?

DORANTE
Well, his own father is Menander.

GERONTE
No, not his father's name, but *his!*

DORANTE
Philander.

GERONTE
Philander! There! Was that so hard?

DORANTE
No harm done.

GERONTE
(Starts out, comes back immediately.)
But wait. It was another name. *Armidon.*
You told me —

DORANTE
Armidon's his *nom de guerre,*
His nickname from the war. He doesn't care,
Himself, how you address him, either name,
Philander, Armidon, it's all the same.
Philander'd be more proper, or more normal.

GERONTE
In my day we preferred to be more formal.
Philander, then. Goodbye.
(GERONTE exits.)

DORANTE
You note how deftly I danced out of *that?*

CLITON
You better write these names inside your hat.

DORANTE
My wits will weave what memory can't supply.
(LUCRECE and ISABELLE leave the window.)

CLITON
O, teach me, master! Teach me how to lie!

DORANTE
Teach you to lie...? But lying is an art.

CLITON
I'm constipated from the truth. Truth's a fart!
O, please, please, please?

DORANTE
All right. Here's where you start:
All the world's a lie, and all the men and women
Merely liars, for each of them must play...

CLITON
A part?

DORANTE

A role. This world's a scrim, Cliton, a fiction,
A richly tapestried, inch-thick depiction
Stretched over some mysterious cosmic hole.
You say that you're a servant. How do I know?
Who's she, or he? Who is the whole back row?
How do I know the smallest thing? I can't.
No one knows anything. So people rant,
Protest, despair, take up astrology —
For each man fears in his biology
That life's a fraud, a fake, an empty vial.
Why else do people primp and pose? *Denial.*
That's where the liar comes in. Because he *knows*
The truth, accepts the void, because he shows
Us the absurd commedia we're all masked for.

CLITON

Ya know, this may be more than what I asked for.

DORANTE

He turns to poetry our daily prose,
Assembles like a magpie some of this
And some of this, a girl, a rose, a kiss,
Expends his magic, his dark artistry,
To dazzle us, reweave the tapestry
With brilliant colors from his endless spools.
He does what Nature does with Nature's tools,
For in a world where priests and princes lie
The liar blends in like a butterfly
As he, in balance with the cosmic fiction,
Persuades us doubting fools through mere conviction.
Now ask me something. Quiz me. I'm at bat.

CLITON

You mean...?

DORANTE

Just try to catch me out. C'mon, chat.

CLITON

So where you from?

DORANTE

Japan.

CLITON
I didn't know *that!*

DORANTE
You see? Conviction.

CLITON
Man!

DORANTE
An air of ease.

CLITON
I half-expected you'd speak Japanese!

DORANTE
Again.

CLITON
I'm gonna get you this time.

DORANTE
Try.

CLITON
Nice weather, huh?

DORANTE
I feel a drop...

CLITON
So do I!
Damn it.

DORANTE
(Peers at Cliton's face.)
What's that...?

CLITON
Where...

DORANTE
Nothing. Just a pimple.

CLITON
A zit?! — God *damn* it!

DORANTE
Lying is so simple.

First: natural gestures. Keep your gravity low,
And centered.
(Hunches slightly, his weight low.)
                    See that? Everything must flow.

CLITON

("Flowing":)
So flow.

DORANTE

            Most vital is the optic nerve.
Engage me.
(Points into his eyes.)
                    Don't allow your gaze to swerve.

CLITON

Don't swerve.

DORANTE

                An easy tone, but with some verve.
So speak your speeches trippingly upon the tongue.

CLITON

(A rippling gesture before his face.)
Tripping.

DORANTE

        Let truth be told, but let your lies be sung.

CLITON

(Bursts into lusty song.)
With verve!

DORANTE

                Irrelevant details are key.
(Tosses it off:)
"It was the tenth of May at six-oh-three..."

CLITON

Gripping.

DORANTE

            But sprinkle in some poetry.
(Airy gesture:)
"The bluebells were just fading now forsooth..."
And lastly — never, ever speak the truth.

CLITON

Lie.

DORANTE

So. Sum up the principles of lying.

CLITON

I can't remember.

DORANTE

Are you lying?

CLITON

No, I'm trying

To get them back!

DORANTE

That's very good! That's great!

CLITON

But I'm not lying yet, I'm — ! Wait, wait, wait.
I got it. Principles of lying.

DORANTE

Go.

CLITON

(A gesture for each, rippling, airy, flowing, etc.)
Don't swerve. Be tripping. Poetry. Stay low.
Irrelevant details. With verve. But flow.

DORANTE

And — ?

CLITON

Never, ever tell the truth.

DORANTE

Bravò,
Cliton, bravò! You see how much you've mastered?

CLITON

Who, me?

DORANTE

You *liar.*

CLITON

Oh, I'm a lying bastard!

C'mon, ask me anything.

DORANTE
Where are you from?

CLITON
Paris. *Japan.*

DORANTE
Wow.

CLITON
Smooth, huh?

DORANTE
I succumbed.

What city?

CLITON
Oh, you know...

DORANTE
Tokyo?

CLITON
Shanghai.

DORANTE
Brilliant. Now get thee forth and multip-lie.

CLITON
But getting back to plot, sir. You don't fret
That your most recent lie's the diciest yet?

DORANTE
Another rung upon my amorous ladder.
And here's a maiden who can aid the matter.
(ISABELLE enters.)
Dear girl, in my transported attitude
I sadly failed to show my gratitude
When last we met. Well, scrimping's not my form.
I live to give. I am a fructifying storm.
I drench the hills, I inundate the plains.
Ask him. (Be quiet.) I shower the earth with rains.
(Takes out a coin.)
So here's a golden raindrop for your pains.

ISABELLE

O, sir, I must decline. I couldn't.

DORANTE

Yes, you must!

After the things you've done?

ISABELLE

I'd be unjust.

CLITON

(Aside to ISABELLE:)
(What's all this garbage, "Sir, I must decline"?)

ISABELLE

(Butt out, pal. You make your rains, I'll make mine.)

DORANTE

(Takes out another coin.)
A second raindrop?

ISABELLE

(Takes the money.)

Sir, I'll tell you all:

It's definite. My lady's in your thrall.
She stayed up half the night because of you.
If you ask me, she's half in love with you.

CLITON

(You musta met the other half last night.)

ISABELLE

She can't *admit* she loves you, out of spite.
Those lies you lavished at the Twillery?
Four years a captain of artillery?
And what about Clarice?

DORANTE

Clarice?

ISABELLE

That suit?

DORANTE

I never sought Clarice. That suit is moot.

ISABELLE

My rainbarrel holds another ounce or two.

DORANTE
You mean...?

ISABELLE
I might have something here for you...
(She takes out a book and dangles it before his eyes.)

DORANTE
Good God! That's not...?!

ISABELLE
Lucrece's private journal.
Now what was that about a rainshower, Colonel?

DORANTE
(Tosses coins.)
O Bella, Bella, buy yourself a gold umbrella!
(He grabs the book and reads.)

ISABELLE
(To CLITON:)
Hello again.

CLITON
Oh, now you recognize me?

ISABELLE
Why wouldn't I?

CLITON
(Offers his cheek to be slapped.)
Okay. C'mon. Tenderize me.
Do it. Right there. Let fly.

ISABELLE
You are so hot.

CLITON
(My chance to lie! Let's take a shot.
Don't swerve. Be tripping. Poetry. Stay low.
Irrelevant details. With *verve!* And flow.)
("Flowing":)
As I was saying, my name's Cliton. *Cliticcup.*

ISABELLE
"Clitoncliticcup"?

CLITON

Yeah, that little hiccup
Is the traditional pronunciation.
Not too uncommon in my family's station.

ISABELLE

What is your station?

CLITON

Oh, Grand Central, down the...
I mean, so do you often stand around the...
Where are we?

ISABELLE

Place Royale.

CLITON

The Place Duluth?

ISABELLE

This is the Place Royale.

CLITON

The hell with truth!
Besides, I just arrived here from Peru.
My goldmines.

ISABELLE

Are you lying?

CLITON

Yes, are you?
Now ask me anything. Ask where I'm from.

ISABELLE

Nice weather, huh?

CLITON

Japan. Well, that was dumb.
D'ya feel a drop?

ISABELLE

No.

CLITON

No?

ISABELLE
What are you, simple?

CLITON
Say, what's that there? Is that a pimple?
(She slaps him.)

CLITON
That's it! I'm swearing off!

DORANTE
(Finishes reading.)
>Read this, my friend, and smile.
It's love! Lucrece is a Dorantophile.

CLITON
You sure it's her?

DORANTE
>The style, Cliton, the style.
She's won. She's mine. Enraptured and resistless.
Isabelle, take this letter to your mistress.
(Gives ISABELLE the letter and returns the book.)

ISABELLE
Yes, sir.

DORANTE
(Gives money.)
>Here's rain until the next installment.

ISABELLE
Yes, *sir!*

DORANTE
>Report my uttermost enthrallment.
(ISABELLE exits.)

CLITON
(Holds out hand.)
I wouldn't mind a small emolument.

DORANTE
I'd better freshen up.

CLITON
>Forget your honey.
SPARE CHANGE?

DORANTE

It's love! I don't have time for money.

(DORANTE starts out. CLITON follows, hand still out. As they go...)

CLITON

They ain't mutually exclusive, ya know.

DORANTE

Later, Cliton, later...

CLITON

You promise?

DORANTE

I promise!

(They're gone.)

Scene Two.

(Lucrece's drawing room. LUCRECE and ISABELLE.)

LUCRECE
So *tell* me, Isabelle. What did he *say?*

ISABELLE
You mean the master, or the weird valet?

LUCRECE
Either.

ISABELLE
He's yours.

LUCRECE
He loves me?

ISABELLE
Love? He's fiery.
But did you need to slip this guy your diary?
(She gives the book back to LUCRECE.)

LUCRECE
I had to test him. See he felt the same.
I still don't quite believe him. There's some *game...*
Or do I fear love? Am I just perverse?
Do *you* believe him?

ISABELLE
I believe his purse.

LUCRECE
Izzy. You didn't take some filthy *bribe?*

ISABELLE
Oh, yes. What better proof that you two jibe?
In this town, gold decides where north and south is,
So love will put its money where its mouth is.

LUCRECE
It's shameful. As if love were born from banks.

ISABELLE
(Takes it out.)
I have a letter from him.

LUCRECE

(Snatches the letter.)

Here's ten francs.

ISABELLE

What shall I say to him about his love note?
I'll say: it flew like pigeon to its dovecote.

LUCRECE

No. Say I tore the letter up unread.

ISABELLE

Oh, brilliant. You prefer to stay unwed?

LUCRECE

Tell him I shredded it with tranquil hands.

ISABELLE

Then goodbye raindrops, hello desert sands.

LUCRECE

Of course, mix in a sweetener, or three...

ISABELLE

"My lady loved your note, it's now debris" — ?

LUCRECE

Oh, you know what I mean. Blame women's nature.
Invest your text with sexist nomenclature.

ISABELLE

We're *moody*. Flighty.

LUCRECE

But in time we soften.
Imply that I might meet him, now and...

ISABELLE

Often.

LUCRECE

I can't just *yield*. That would be insane.
I want to crack the door...

ISABELLE

...but leave it on the chain?

I've played this field.
(ISABELLE exits.)

LUCRECE

Tell him I tore it up! — Where was I now...
(Scans letter.)
"Joyrapturetransporthappiness *accept my vow*
Of love." He loves me. Me, Lucrece! But *how,*
How could Apollo stoop to such as I?
And yet he seems to droop as much as I.
"Agonysorrowanguishtorment *how I've yearned*
For you." That proves it, far as I'm concerned.
And yet it's odd how he extols my eyes.
He hasn't seen them! "*Lazuli at sunrise*,"
He calls them. Lovely. So why analyze
What he... Yet here he says "Your lips, your face..."
He hasn't seen those either. "Your embrace
Is all I crave." I really have to shred this.
(She holds it as if to tear it up.)
Be brave, Lucrece. Well, after I've reread this,
Where is it, here, "Your delicate, warm hand
So pliant to my touch..." *Delicate hand...*
Hmm. Well, *that*, now, I don't understand.
How could he know my hand is pliable?
The letter's really unreliable.
"Blahblahblahblah *your voice*, each note a pearl."
He's never heard it! All right, who's this girl
He's writing to? It's somebody, but who..?
(CLARICE enters, followed by SABINE.)

CLARICE

Lucy, let me embrace you! What a morning!
A miracle!

LUCRECE

What's happened?

CLARICE

Without warning
I find myself amidst the Great Event!

LUCRECE

You're pregnant?

CLARICE

No! Al's father came from Ghent!

LUCRECE

So you can marry!

CLARICE

Well...

LUCRECE

What's this? Why frown?

CLARICE

We have to wait.

LUCRECE

For what?

CLARICE

My uncle to come down.
But once he does, we'll set the wedding date!
(Jubilation.)

LUCRECE

You were so worried. This should compensate.

CLARICE

Compensate? How?

LUCRECE

For having lost Dorante.

CLARICE

Ha, ha, ha, ha! Monsieur Dorante, the vaunted?
I never sought him. You're the one he wanted.
That's all dead wood now. I called him a beast.
Sabine?

SABINE

You did, Miss. Fifty times at least.

CLARICE

I'm only glad I got to get his goat.

LUCRECE

He just wrote *me* the most affecting note...

CLARICE

Oh, poor Lucrece. You don't believe this boy?
(Takes letter.)
"Joy, rapture..." Every word is pure trompe l'oeil!

LUCRECE

You don't say this, I'm sure, because he scorned you.

CLARICE

Believe him. Fine. Remember that I warned you.

LUCRECE

You think this isn't love, and I'm a sap?
All this is desperation?

CLARICE

It's a trap.
This isn't *love*, Lucrece! You're simply curious!

LUCRECE

If you and I weren't best friends, I'd be furious.
But let's stop here. Why hack through this "dead wood"?

CLARICE

Well, fine.

LUCRECE

We're understood.

CLARICE

How've *you* been?

LUCRECE

Good.

We're friends again?

CLARICE

Oh, Lucy...

LUCRECE

It's so *stupid*!

(They laugh about it all.)
Yet yesterday you acted like this boy was Cupid
And now there's all this animosity.
So was that love, or "curiosity"?

CLARICE

Mere curiosity. A chance to laugh!
I *listened*, yes, awaiting some dumb gaffe.

LUCRECE

Just as I read this note. Amused. Aloof.
I read it as one takes some silly spoof.

"Agonysorrowanguishtorment..."
I'm going to rip it up. The whole thing's spurious.

CLARICE
(Takes the letter.)
I don't see why you should, if you're just curious.

LUCRECE
Following your example, my wise friend.

CLARICE
(Hands it back.)
Well, then, let rip!

LUCRECE
(Hands it back.)
      I will!

CLARICE
(Hands it back.)
       Ta-ta!

LUCRECE
(Rips it up.)
          The end!

CLARICE
Of course, to listen simply means you're civil.
Reading a note you lend yourself to drivel.

LUCRECE
Claire...

CLARICE
I just don't want you left in some man's lurch.

LUCRECE
You know what I think? We should go to church.

CLARICE
A wonderful idea!

LUCRECE
      Let's hear Mass,
Then we'll forget that cad.

CLARICE
      That liar.

LUCRECE
That ass.

SABINE
Are you two mad? Have you both lost the drift?
Madame, the gods have blessed you with a gift!
Do we so often yearn, so often burn
With passion for a man, that we should spurn
Him when he comes, or let him cause a rift,
However shifty this man's bent might be?
Hear this: each man's imperfect. So are we.

LUCRECE
Sabine...!

SABINE
Good Christ, madame, *pursue* this youth!
Go now. Go find Dorante, surrender couth,
And wring from him what he thinks is the truth!

LUCRECE
Yes, Miss.

CLARICE
Yes, Miss.

SABINE
Now move!
(All exit.)

Scene Three.

(The Place Royale. GERONTE enters as PHILISTE enters opposite, carrying a bouquet. PHILISTE heads for Clarice's house.)

GERONTE

What, is that you, Philiste?

PHILISTE
Monsieur.

GERONTE
Well met.

You know Poitiers.

PHILISTE
My birthplace.

GERONTE
Better yet.

Acquainted as you are — and in all candor —
Apprize me all you can about Philander.

PHILISTE

Phil...

GERONTE
...ander. From your home locality.

Just any facts. His personality,
His family, his fortune, fealty, fame....

PHILISTE

I'll tell you all: I've never heard the name.

GERONTE

You mean...? Well, yes, small wonder how you stare.
To you he's Armidon! His *nom de guerre*.
The father of Orphise? Whose beauty ranks
As high as snow upon the Pyrenees?

PHILISTE

No slander on Philander. Both are blanks.
(Turns to leave.)

GERONTE

Ah-ha! Such tact. You're sheltering my boy.
You've sworn to keep hush-hush about his joy.
Well, I know all. The watch, the pistol shot,

Her father forcing him to tie the knot...

PHILISTE
You mean Dorante has wed? Is this a jest?

GERONTE
He's young, he's mine, I heard, I acquiesced.

PHILISTE
But — married? He?

GERONTE
     Here's more, if you're beguiled.
The two of them are going to have a child.

PHILISTE
Who told you this?

GERONTE
    Why, he himself! Dorante!

PHILISTE
Ah. Should have guessed. The story's so piquant.

GERONTE
You mean to cast some doubt upon this tale?

PHILISTE
No, no. He has a gift in proud, full sail —
Your son's this world's most brilliant adapter.
No doubt in time he'll add another chapter,
Detailed, delicious, packed with derring-do —
At sea, perhaps, with magic herring, too.
He conjured some imaginary food.
No doubt Orphise was born of this same brood.

GERONTE
I'll break your neck. I'll put your legs in splints!

PHILISTE
He must have shown you proofs, you're so convinced.
A portrait, or a license — ?

GERONTE
    Well, no...

PHILISTE
      Hell, no.

As for this grandchild waiting at the sill,
I'll say but this: *I wouldn't change my will.*
Adieu.
(PHILISTE exits.)

GERONTE

A man of my age, taken by surprise.
Was it a dream, a cloud of buzzing lies,
This world I've walked in, blunt and sound as rock?
Myself I find turned to a laughingstock!
O wicked. Dastardly. Unkind. Felonious!
(DORANTE enters, followed by CLITON.)

GERONTE

Are you a gentleman?

DORANTE

(Oh, no. Polonius.)
A gentleman? Of course I am, being thine.

GERONTE

You think that that's enough? To share my line?
Well, in the sink of lies you're swimming in,
As King of France you'd be no gentleman!

DORANTE

Has someone said I lied?

GERONTE

Has someone *said?*
It's printed here in bold across your head!
Remind me, if you can, of your wife's name.

DORANTE

Her name...?

GERONTE

Her name, boy. Can you tell me that?

CLITON

(I told you, write these names inside your hat.)

GERONTE

Perhaps her father's name, or his estate?
Come, dazzle me. Invent a potentate!
Is he the King of Prussia? Duc de Guise?

CLITON
(Engage him. Use the optic nerve.)

DORANTE
(Quiet, please.)

GERONTE
Do you recall the name *Orphise?*

DORANTE
Orphise.

GERONTE
What spawned such lies? Betrothal to Clarice?
You turned your father, because of this niece,
Into a senile fool, your shill, your goat?
Why? Did I hold a dagger to your throat?
Why artifice? The watch, the gun, that anthem.
I blessed your marriage to a gypsy phantom,
How could you doubt I'd give my fond consent
To a flamingo, so you were content?
You've shown a loving father neither fear,
Respect, nor love. What *have* you shown? A sneer.
I wish to God I'd never bred nor known you.
So go, my son no more. I now disown you.

DORANTE
The truth is...

GERONTE
Truth! Will your lips let it pass?
The truth fits you as false teeth fit an ass.

CLITON
Hee-haw!

DORANTE
You see, I've met this girl... No, this one's real.
Her name's Lucrece, and she's my heart's ideal.

GERONTE
I knew her mother well. A royal Briton...

DORANTE
The moment that I met her I was smitten.

GERONTE

And that was — ?

DORANTE

Yesterday. No, wait. Please listen.
So unacquainted how could I reveal
My love to you, not knowing how she'd feel?
But now she's written. Read this tender piece.
(Shows letter.)
I had to shed the yoke of dread Clarice,
So, yes, I shammed, I told a thousand lies,
But now I beg, by every knot that ties,
Support me in my suit.

GERONTE

Would that be wise?
If you're deceiving me —

DORANTE

You're still in doubt?
Believe Cliton. He knows me inside out.

GERONTE

Yes, after this extravagant ballet
I'll trust some lying, fraudulent valet?

CLITON

(Why, I oughta...)
(DORANTE holds him back.)

GERONTE

Well, I'm a reasonable man, and just.
I'll see her father and attempt his trust.
But if I find that this is all some trick,
If your words and reality don't click,
I swear by these wide rays that lighten men
My sword will vouch you never lie again.
You'll couch here pooled in blood while honor stands
With justice rendered by this father's hands.
Jove, I have vowed it!
(GERONTE exits.)

CLITON

He'll kill you.

DORANTE

          I doubt it.

CLITON

Frankly, monsieur, you disappointed me.
You got him twice. I hoped you'd go for three.

DORANTE

Cliton, there's something nagging like a tooth.

CLITON

Remorse, perhaps, for having told the truth?
Or maybe that was all another wheeze
And you don't really love the fair Lucreze.

DORANTE

No, no. I *do*. At least — I *think* I do...

CLITON

You THINK?

DORANTE

          Well, how should *I* know if it's true?
I've lied to everyone. To him. To you.
It's like I've grown this lying, inner elf.
What if my elf is lying to my self?
What if it isn't love, and I'm an ijjit?

CLITON

Hey, don't ask me. Consult your inner midget.

DORANTE

Look at her friend. That minx?

CLITON

          You mean the sphinx?

DORANTE

How can I trust, should that girl ever speak,
That I won't fall for *her* within the week?
She had a certain grace and style and air.
Stand the two side by side, she's just as fair.
And she exuded such a *je ne sais quoi!*

CLITON

Back then you said she had a *je ne sais blah.*

DORANTE

Because she bothered me.

CLITON

Sure. Sheer frustration.

DORANTE

No, no, Cliton. Incipient fascination.

CLITON

Small detail? You forget that girl is took.

DORANTE

Alcippe.

CLITON

Alcippe.

DORANTE

Thank God! I'm off the hook!
Well, fine. I'll love Lucrece. Given the situation.

CLITON

What is this, process of elimination?
And if you doubted, why pile on more lies?
Your Dad just heard you praise her to the skies.

DORANTE

He wouldn't have believed me otherwise.

CLITON

You sent him for her hand! You've tied the loop!

DORANTE

A holding action. Now I can regroup.

CLITON

Regroup? You're running out of options, fella!

DORANTE

Never. And look, here comes fair Isabella.
(ISABELLE enters.)

ISABELLE

Monsieur.

DORANTE

You gave my note? She vetted it?

ISABELLE

Not quite.

DORANTE

You mean...

ISABELLE

I mean she shredded it.
She ripped it into strips, then bits, then glitter.
In short, she quickly made your letter litter.

DORANTE

You *let* her?

ISABELLE

Sir, my lady came unglued!
She's going to fire me.

CLITON

Okay, now you're screwed.

ISABELLE

And yet...

DORANTE

And yet — ?

ISABELLE

My hand has such a thirst...

DORANTE

(Gives more money.)
And yet?

ISABELLE

She shredded it, but read it first.
Indeed, sir, she as good as memorized it.

DORANTE

You're lying.

ISABELLE

This is *truth!*

DORANTE

Well, I can't recognize it!

ISABELLE

I see her coming with Clarice in tow.

Good luck, monsieur. You still may be her beau —
If not her husband.
(ISABELLE exits.)

DORANTE
"If not her husband..."?

DORANTE & CLITON
Whoa!
(LUCRECE and CLARICE enter, followed by SABINE.)

CLARICE
(Be strong. Speak out. No sidelong looks. No peeking.)

LUCRECE
(But if he lies?)

CLARICE
(You'll know.)

LUCRECE
(How?)

CLARICE
(He'll be speaking.)

LUCRECE
Monsieur...

DORANTE
You've come at last to grant my suit!
Let's cast aside all doubt, let's face the truth.
(Walking past LUCRECE to CLARICE.)
Until you are my bride I will not rest.
(He kisses CLARICE's hand. Over his bowed head:)

CLARICE
(You'd think that it was *me* whom he addressed.)

LUCRECE
(It must be nerves.)

CLARICE
(No doubt.)

LUCRECE
Monsieur...

DORANTE
(To CLARICE, ignoring LUCRECE:)
                                        Without
Your rays, your sunshine, how am I to be?

CLARICE
(His gaze appears to be affixed on me.)

LUCRECE
(A stray glance hit you, inadvertently.)
Monsieur Dorante...

DORANTE
(Follows CLARICE around.)
                        And if today I languished,
Two days without you would be utter anguish.   .
A year, a hell. How could I bear a life?
Therefore I ask again. Pray, be my wife!
(He throws himself down and follows CLARICE on his knees.)

CLARICE
(He pointed that at me. You did remark it?)

LUCRECE
(Perhaps if you stood wider of the target.)

CLARICE
(Stood wider of the target? I'm his aim!)

LUCRECE
Monsieur Dorante —

DORANTE
(To CLARICE:)
                        I love you!

LUCRECE
                                (It's some game.)

CLARICE
(Why?)

LUCRECE
            (*I* don't know! Perhaps to twist our plight
He chases you by day and me by night!)

CLARICE
(He's on his knees! I think he's plopped for *me!*)

LUCRECE
(Shows the bits of her letter.)
(And what about his note? Exhibit B?)

DORANTE
If I might interrupt. Your friend, madame,
Who otherwise is something of a clam,
Has found her tongue. I bear her no bad will,
But she has private cause to wish me ill.

LUCRECE
(A *CLAM*? I'll kill him. I'll rip out his nails.)

CLARICE
My friend has told me certain curious tales...

DORANTE
The troubled fancies of a jealous mind.
Your maid can tell you how my own's inclined.
(To SABINE:)
Just say it in the simplest words you can.

SABINE
I've had no conversations with this man.

DORANTE
She's mad!

CLARICE
(He's mad.)

LUCRECE
(He's mad.)

CLITON
(To SABINE:)
You're *mad!*

CLARICE
Sir, you do recognize me? Know this face?

DORANTE
Good God, I'd have to be from outer space.
You whom I met near here just yesterday?
Whose hand I held, who — ?

CLARICE
Skip the resume.

Blah, blah, blah. I'm your goddess, you're my slave.
But there's not someone *else* whose love you crave?

DORANTE

No! It's for you and you alone I swoon.

CLARICE

You said you'd rather wed a dead baboon.

DORANTE

Forget the ape! My feelings are profounder.
If I can't marry you, I'd rather wed a flounder!

CLITON

(Nice one.)

CLARICE

Lucrece, a word.

DORANTE

(Lucrece?!)

CLITON

(Lucrece?!)

DORANTE

(You heard?)

CLITON

(I said she was Lucrece. You wouldn't budge.
Okay, now, smart guy — who's the better judge?)

DORANTE

(But last night at the gate...)

CLITON

(The switcheroo.)

DORANTE

(One played the other...)

CLITON

(...and you pitched her woo.)

DORANTE

(But what about the maid who wouldn't tell?)

CLARICE

Sabine, find Isabelle.

(SABINE exits.)

CLITON
(Sabine?)

DORANTE
(Sabine? And Isabelle?)

CLITON
(And Isabelle?)
(ISABELLE enters and waves coyly to CLITON.)

CLITON
(Well, that explains it.)

DORANTE & CLITON
(Twin from hell!)

CLARICE
Monsieur Dorante.

DORANTE
Madame?

CLARICE
My friend "The Clam"
Has told me all, and of your shameful sham.
Did you not court this girl with praise profuse
While heaping me with nothing but abuse?

DORANTE
I'm sorry, when was this?

CLARICE
Oh, you're so slick.

DORANTE
No, really, madam. Are you playing a trick?

CLARICE
Last night! What chasm is your memory cursed with?

DORANTE
But you're the only lady I've conversed with.

CLARICE
You didn't speak to her last night till two?

DORANTE

How could I — speaking as I was to *you?*

CLARICE

Me...?

DORANTE

You. You thought I wouldn't know your voice?

CLARICE

So you...?

DORANTE

Madame, you left me little choice
But to indulge your clever masquerade.
You played Lucrece, I played the courtly blade,
And just to baffle you in your attempt,
Each time you said "Clarice," I feigned contempt.

CLARICE

And your imaginary marriage meant —
What, when your father'd come to seek my hand?

DORANTE

My bogus bride helped wrap a wedding band
Around your finger, just as I had planned.

CLARICE

(Shows her bare finger.)
What band?

DORANTE

I thought you'd bought your bridal gown...

CLARICE

I will — once Uncle What's-His-Name comes down.

DORANTE

In any case, Alcippe need never know
You met in secret with another beau.
Alcippe's so sensitive. Protect him, will you?

LUCRECE

Well, speaking for *The Clam*, I still could kill you!
Oh, yes, it's well and good to speak of "fun."
Clarice? Clarice is not the only one
To like some fun. I like fun, too. I love it!

My name's Lucrece. But your fun, sir, well *shove* it's
What *I* say. *Shove* it! For while you were aching
With laughter, certain hearts were busy breaking.
I speak of mine, sir. Mine. Your loving oyster.
The bivalve at the back whose eyes grew moister
At the mere mention of your name. What prize,
What goal could you have gained from all those lies,
And from entangling me in your wild skein?
Why write me, for example, this long strain,
Apparently sincere, on your devotion?
(Takes out the bits of his letter.)
It breaks my heart to hold it. What an ocean,
What a wide, warm sea I rode when reading it.
What malice must have gone to breeding it.
But was it malice? Here, sir, have a piece.
Have all. But answer: was it mere caprice?

DORANTE
My goal was simple. To win *you*, Lucrece.

CLARICE
Don't tell me you *believe* that...

LUCRECE
                        Peace, Clarice.

DORANTE
You lent your friend your name and garden lawn
To stage her fraudulent *divertissement*,
And doing so became one of her engines.
You tortured me, I had my petty vengeance.
Forgive a lover, wounded but devout.

LUCRECE
And at the Twillery? You seemed to flout
Me, bantering with her. Was that mirage?

DORANTE
You might say that Clarice was camouflage.
She may have shared my words. You shared my heart.

CLARICE
Now this is magic of the highest art.
It's smoke and mirrors, Lucy. Sleight-of-hand.

DORANTE

I'm so in love I'm out of sight of land.

LUCRECE

Yes, with a mollusk, thank you. Not a girl.

DORANTE

A mollusk at whose middle lies a pearl.
And you may be a bivalve, but you're *my* valve.
Lucrece, I swear...

CLARICE

I swear, this man's a tease!

DORANTE

Let me not to the marriage —

LUCRECE

No Shakespeare, please!

DORANTE

You're right. You're right. I know *that's* always true.
It takes a liar to know a girl like you —
Whose gaze illumines me and makes me blush.
Forgive me, madam, that I did not rush
Into your arms the morning that we met:
What women know, men can take years to get.
Pardon my truancy, forgive my timing.
To make it clear, I'll say it without rhyming:
(Very simply:)
I love you, Lucrece. Whatever any man could hope for in a
woman is in you. Beauty, tenderness, intelligence, amazing
tits, I didn't mean that, passion, honesty, morality, the kind
that can move even an idiot like me. You are what most men
only dream of. I say all this without knowing you very well.
In fact, I don't know you literally at all, except about your ski
chalet and your father's name, which I can't remember. You see
how honest I'm being? These have been the most wonderful
twenty-nine hours of my life! The hours that included you, I
mean. Please, Lucrece, please let me try to deserve you. If you
try to love me maybe I can grow up into the kind of man who's
worthy of your infinite perfections. And your amazing tits.
Yes? No? Yes? Dear God, I hope that you believe me *now*.

LUCRECE
Well... *WOW.* But...

DORANTE
If you still doubt, ask my *chargé d'affaires.*
(To CLITON:)
Did I not praise her style and grace and air?
Her *je ne sais quoi?*

CLITON
I swear — as God is law!

ISABELLE
And madam, this valet's veracity
Matches his master's late mendacity.
Monsieur Dorante is really fiercely fond.

LUCRECE
Yes, but the facts and he don't correspond!

DORANTE
But if I say my father, as we speak,
Has gone to yours, dispatched by me to seek
Your hand — would that prove my sincerity?

LUCRECE
It might — unless some fresh disparity
Pops your soufflé.

DORANTE
But look — Pop's on his way.
(GERONTE enters.)

GERONTE
The match is made, so set your mind at ease.
We only need the say-so of Orphise.

LUCRECE
Orphise?! Who's she?

GERONTE
Lucrece, I mean. Apologies.
Too many brides. So you're the Aphrodite
Who's captured my son's heart?

LUCRECE
Well, sir. I might be —

Depending.

GERONTE
But it all depends on you!
See how my puppy bends his eye on you?
He's faithful, youthful... Sorry, have we met?

LUCRECE
Yes, at your puppy's previous marital *fête*.

GERONTE
Well, will you have him? Join the family phylum?
Or shall I take a cell in some asylum?

LUCRECE
Good sir, I have good reasons to revile him.
The reasons, like Dorante, are convolute.
But heart says love, and heart I can't refute.
I'll take him — *and* his brilliant little jokes.
(DORANTE and LUCRECE kiss.)

GERONTE
Looks like a marriage made in heaven, folks!

ALCIPPE
(Offstage:)
Clarice! *Clarice!*
(ALCIPPE enters with PHILISTE.)

ALCIPPE
Your uncle says it all depends on you!

CLARICE
Time out while I experience *déja vu*.

ALCIPPE
Well? Yes or no? Don't stand there like some statue!
Oh, sweetie.

CLARICE
Pug, what man on earth can match you?
Of course I'll have you!
(ALCIPPE and CLARICE kiss.)

GERONTE
Blessings on you all!

PHILISTE

One second! I, too, stand in someone's thrall.
(Pulls ISABELLE to him.)
Sabine, my queen, let's do it. Let's elope!

CLITON

(Pulling ISABELLE back.)
Sorry, pal. This queen's Isabelle. I hope...
(CLITON is about to kiss ISABELLE.)

PHILISTE

Isabelle...?

CLITON

What, do you mean you didn't know —
The duo status of the status quo?
G'wan, show him, babe.

ISABELLE

(Exiting:)

Sabine!

CLITON

You'll think they fake it.

PHILISTE

You mean...?

CLITON

Buck up now. See if you can take it.
(He does a drum roll, and SABINE enters.)

SABINE

Philiste!

PHILISTE

Sabine...?

SABINE

I didn't think I'd make it.

PHILISTE

You mean...?!

CLITON

Hey, talk about your *je ne sais quoi!*

PHILISTE

Sabine — ??!!

CLITON

Your very own *ménage à trois!*

SABINE

Rrrrrr!
(SABINE wraps PHILISTE in a passionate kiss.)

DORANTE

My friends, here's to my Dad, without whose virtue
I'd not have known how fraudulence can hurt you!
(GERONTE begins to sob loudly.)
But father, what's the matter? Why these tears?

GERONTE

Oh, how I've lied, I've lied for all these years!
This show of probity that's masked my sin!
To have begot, and then forgot, your twin!

DORANTE

My twin — ?

GERONTE

A tale far taller than your fakery.
I left him with some crullers in a bakery!
The source, of course, of many a marital scrimmage.
Like you he has a birthmark in the image
Of a red rooster, crowing on his tongue.

CLITON

A what?

GERONTE

That's how I'd know that he's my young.
By that lost bird.

CLITON

Yeah, but — *my* tongue has always sung. See
that?
(Sticks out his tongue.)

GERONTE

Dorante, you heard?
(DORANTE sticks out his tongue, too.)
Two cocks — of matching colors!

CLITON

Not only that.
(Produces them.)

I've got your missing crullers!

GERONTE

Chanticleer's crowed! The truth has finally won!

CLITON

Are you my Dad?

GERONTE

Come greet your papa, son!
(GERONTE and CLITON embrace.)

ALL

Awww.

GERONTE

Have half my all, plus what comes from your mother.
Now happy truth — embrace your lying brother.
(DORANTE and CLITON embrace.)

ALL

Awww.

DORANTE

(To us:)
How liars are punishéd by their own lies!
Was *not* the moral of this exercise
But rather how, amidst life's contradictions,
Our lives can far out-fick the finest fictions.
A son and brother spun from a valet,
Four marriages at once (with ski chalet).
The other warps and wooves within this matrix,
Twin sets of twins, a blushing dominatrix.
Yes, sometimes life is lively, sometimes duller,
Sometimes it's cruel, sometimes a missing cruller.
What things aren't possible in God's creation!
(With a small push from the imagination.)
And I? Well, given how sham's my benefactor,
Perhaps I'll go onstage and be an actor.
Maybe Corneille will write me up a play.
Or maybe, given my gifts and disposition,
I'll emigrate and be a politician.

But think, before you hit the parking booth,
How this was all a lie — and yet the truth.
Impossible? Don't hurt your spinning head.
Just hie thee happily home and lie — in bed!

END OF PLAY